A.L.I.E.N.S.
Awakened Lives Invading Every Nation Supernaturally

By
Rohan Peart

Watersprings
PUBLISHING

A.L.I.E.N.S. published by Watersprings Publishing House, LLC., P.O. Box 1284 Olive Branch, MS 38654
www.waterspringspublishing.com. Contact the publisher for bulk orders and permission requests.

Copyright © 2024 ROHAN PEART. All rights reserved. No part of this publication may be reproduced, distributed, or transmitted in any form or by any means, including photocopying, recording, or other electronic or mechanical methods, without the prior written permission of the publisher, except in the case of brief quotations embodied in critical reviews and certain other noncommercial uses permitted by copyright law.

Scripture quotations marked "ESV" are taken from The Holy Bible, English Standard Version. Copyright © 2000; 2001 by Crossway Bibles, a division of Good News Publishers. Used by permission. All rights reserved.

Scripture quotations are taken from the Holy Bible, New International Version®. NIV® Copyright 1973, 1978, 1984 by International Bible Society. Used by permission of Zondervan. All rights reserved.

Scripture quotations marked "NKJV" are taken from the New King James Version. Copyright © 1982 by Thomas Nelson, Inc. Used by permission. All rights reserved.

Scripture quotations marked (NLT) are taken from the Holy Bible, New Living Translation, copyright © 1996. Used by permission of Tyndale House Publishers, Inc., Wheaton, IL 60189 USA. All rights reserved.

Scripture quotations from THE MESSAGE. Copyright © by Eugene H. Peterson 1993, 1994, 1995, 1996, 2000, 2001, 2002. Used by permission of NavPress Publishing Group.

The Voice Bible Copyright © 2012 Thomas Nelson, Inc. The Voice™ translation © 2012 Ecclesia Bible Society All rights reserved.

Scripture quotations marked NLV are taken from the New Life Version, Copyright © 1969 and 2003. Used by permission of Barbour Publishing, Inc., Uhrichsville, Ohio 44683. All rights reserved.

Scriptures marked TLB are taken from the THE LIVING BIBLE (TLB): Scripture taken from THE LIVING BIBLE copyright© 1971. Used by permission of Tyndale House Publishers, Inc., Carol Stream, Illinois 60188. All rights reserved.

Scripture is taken from GOD'S WORD®, © 1995 God's Word to the Nations. Used by permission of Baker Publishing Group.

Printed in the United States of America.

ISBN-13: 979-8-9894494-8-4

I would like to dedicate this book to my family. First to my father, Arlington Peart. Even though he never had an official religious title, I consider him my first Pastor. To my mother, Morrinette Ramocan, for always believing in me and being my first intercessor. To my older sister Trudy, for always having my back, and to my wife Sheretha for being my best friend and life partner. I love you all deeply.

CONTENTS

PREFACE 7

INTRODUCTION 11

CHAPTER 1: ONCE UPON A TIME 15

CHAPTER 2: THE INVASION BEGINS 23

CHAPTER 3: NOT OF THIS WORLD 37

CHAPTER 4: SEEING THE KINGDOM 55

CHAPTER 5: THE FIRST INVASION 75

CHAPTER 6: THE SECOND INVASION 87

CHAPTER 7: THE BEST OF BOTH WORLDS 103

CHAPTER 8: A PRIESTLY KINGDOM 119

CHAPTER 9: THE REAL YOU 139

CHAPTER 10: THY KINGDOM COME 167

LET US PRAY 184

ABOUT THE AUTHOR 185

"...JESUS ANSWERED, "GOD'S KINGDOM IS COMING, BUT NOT IN A WAY THAT YOU WILL BE ABLE TO SEE WITH YOUR EYES. PEOPLE WILL NOT SAY, 'LOOK, HERE IT IS!' OR, 'THERE IT IS!' BECAUSE GOD'S KINGDOM IS WITHIN YOU."
LUKE 17:20-21

PREFACE

OK, I admit it. This is an odd title for a book that has nothing to do with actual aliens from another planet. This is not a book about UFOs, purple creatures from outer space, avatars in indigenous jungles, or men in black. But it *is* a book about aliens. Not the edge-of-your-seat sci-fi flicks that usually come to mind when you hear the word. Not at all. It's something altogether more spectacular than that and yet relatable. It has been all around us since the beginning of time and has existed before time began.

It's the Kingdom of Heaven. That celestial Society of magnificent splendor. The Kingdom of unending justice, peace, and joy. This book is about the heritage, the design, and the responsibility of the citizens born into that heavenly civilization. I must say from the onset that I did not set out to write a book. However, I believe it is quite possible that I spend more time writing than anyone else I know.

Nevertheless, that is not what I initially intended to do. My objective was only to jot down a few of the many revelatory insights that consume my thoughts throughout the day. But this train of thought seemed to take on a life of its own, and this work is the result of it. It's a sermon series that turned into a book.

I truly believe that the words contained in the chapters of this book have the potential to shift the way we think about spiritual things. I can no more take credit for them than I can my ability to inhale and exhale. It really doesn't even feel like I wrote a book. It only feels like I have exhaled onto these pages the glorious truths I have inhaled in God's presence. Without the Holy Spirit whispering in my ear and sharing His thoughts with me, I would still feel very much like the insecure nine-year-old boy I once was, failing Mrs. Marshall's third-grade special education class. Or the 12-year-old boy standing in the office of a doctor, who is telling my mother that I have a neurological dysfunction that would prohibit me from ever being able to articulate myself properly. I believe the reason that God knows He can trust me with this significant revelation is because He knows that I know how incompetent I am without Him. The reason it is important to me that you know that it is God who moved me to write these words is because it is important for you to read it with that in mind. These are not just some clever theological concepts. Rather, these are truths God has revealed to me over the years that have changed the way I see Him, myself, and the world around me. Like the warning labels and placards on trucks, barrels, or boxes in which hazardous materials are contained, I warn you to read this book carefully and prayerfully. If you don't, I believe it will be of no benefit to you.

I give you this caution not because I believe myself to be someone of great importance, in possession of spiritual insights so precious that the masses will never be privy to them. That is not at all the spirit or attitude in which I approach this warning. I rather hope that you receive it in the same spirit in which the Apostle Paul wrote to the Church at Corinth. In 1 Corinthians 3:2, he said, *"I had to feed you with milk, not with solid food because you weren't ready for anything stronger. And you still aren't ready."*

Paul was not reluctant to share the deep things of God with the Corinthian church because he thought them to be uneducated people. In fact, they were quite the opposite. They were a part of a culture that believed in getting the best education they could afford.

And though they weren't as prestigious as those in Athens, they had an insatiable intellectual appetite for philosophical and theological knowledge. His reluctance to share the deep things of God with them was because of his concern for their spiritual readiness to receive it. My concern is not that the content of this book is too deep to understand. It is actually very basic and quite simple. It is rather that these basic and simple truths have the potential to usher the carnal mind into deep places in God that will eventually drown them in things their unrepentant heart wasn't yet ready to receive. I used to Pastor a church in Marietta, Georgia. I remember one day, immediately after one of our worship services, one of the members said, "I love listening to you because you are always so deep!" Though I politely thanked him, I was quite bothered by that statement. I didn't understand why it bothered me so much at first until several hours later. He liked the fact that my teachings were *deep*, but I kept wondering how deep any of those teachings had gone into his heart. I knew this man and the lifestyle he was content with living. Though I wasn't standing in judgment of him, it bothered me that he loved my deep teachings, but he was still content to live a shallow life. Even though his statement bothered me, it was good for me. It caused me to change my perspective on what it really means to be deep. It is not my desire to *be* deep. It is my desire to *go* deep. I desire to take the simple things of God and go to a deeper place in Him. But I never want to go deeper than my spiritual maturity, and God has given me the authorization to go.

So, inspect your heart. Examine your spiritual walk and consider your motives for reading this book. If it's fueled by a sense of readiness to take your spiritual life more seriously and understand just what the Kingdom of Heaven is all about, then keep reading. This book is for you.

ROHAN PEART

GOD HAS PLACED AN APPETITE FOR ETERNAL THINGS IN THE HEART OF EVERY HUMAN BEING.

INTRODUCTION

Long before the 1996 box office smash hit *Independence Day*, the 1982 motion picture *E.T.*, or even before the 1902 French silent film, *A Trip to the Moon*, the Bible recorded the existence of aliens. I'll even take it a step further. Not only has the Bible talked about aliens, but it has also documented a significant number of alien invasions throughout history. Whether it was Moses' invasion of Egypt, the Messiah's invasion of human history, or the Church's invasion of the world system, aliens have always been among us.

In fact, the title of this book, A.L.I.E.N.S., is actually a play on the word. It's an acronym I came up with in preparation to preach a sermon series on ordinary people possessing the supernatural power of God. It stands for:

Anointed
Lives
Invading
Every
Nation
Supernaturally

It also stands for:

Awakened
Lives
Invading
Every
Nation
Supernaturally

To be awakened means to be revived by God with a newfound spiritual awareness. To be anointed means to be chosen and empowered by God.

Whether or not there are extraterrestrial beings that visit our planet in spaceships from time to time is certainly debatable. Since the congressional hearings in the summer of 2023, there has been a widespread belief that the government has been concealing the existence of aliens from outer space. Wherever you stand on that, I believe that God, as the Creator, created much more than we are aware of and much more than our finite minds are able to fathom on this side of eternity. But one thing I do know for sure is the kind of aliens the Bible speaks about are the citizens of the Kingdom of Heaven, anointed and awakened by the Spirit of God, to invade the world with supernatural power.

These are the aliens we'll be examining in this book. The kind every human being has the capacity to become. We'll be taking a closer look at how we are designed by God to be the best of both worlds. Heavenly spirits with earthly bodies. We'll also explore the supernatural nature that is resident within every citizen of the Kingdom of God, and how those who are ambassadors of that Kingdom should be functioning in this world.

From superheroes to vampires, you can't turn on the television lately without seeing an advertisement for an upcoming movie or a network television show about something supernatural. We are so fascinated with the supernatural that, in 2005, there was even a television series called *Supernatural* that ran for 15 seasons. Its season finale was in 2020.

Why this level of demand for sci-fi, outer space, vampire, and superhero movies? Why have books and movies like *Harry Potter, Twilight, The Avengers,* and shows like *True Blood* and *The Walking Dead* been so successful in the last 25 years? I believe the reason we're so intrigued by them is because, subconsciously, we know that some variation of the things we're viewing in these shows are what God originally designed us to be. That is, spiritual and supernatural beings.

The human body is made up of 70 percent water. Therefore, it craves a significant amount of water in order to survive. Your human spirit is 100 percent God; therefore, it craves a significant amount of God in order to survive. Since your spirit consists of more of God than your body consists of water, then your spirit craves God more than your body craves water. Throughout the day, your human body is communicating to you, "I need more water; I need more water." Throughout the day, your spirit communicates, "I need more God, I need more God." Your body comes from the earth and consists of the earth. Therefore, it is designed to exist on the earth, and be continually sustained by the earth. Your spirit comes from God and consists of God. Therefore, it is designed to exist in God and be continually sustained by God. The aspect of us that craves eternity is the aspect of us that is eternal. It's what we crave because it's what we are and where we come from. We can't help it.

Ecclesiastes 3:11

"...God has planted eternity in the human heart."

God has placed an appetite for eternal things in the heart of every human being. So even our overindulgence in anything is born out of our misdirected desire for God. Stephen King's love of horror is his misdirected desire for the Eternity that God has placed in his heart. He, like everyone else, desires to be an alien. Someone sent from the Kingdom of Heaven to bring everything in the sphere of their influence under the authority of that Kingdom. That's the desire that God has placed within his heart. He just doesn't know it. Neither do most of the people driving to and from work, making plans for their future.

There's a longing within them for something more, but they misidentify it as something else. Then, they direct it toward something else. Maybe you do the same thing. Maybe you try to ignore the God factor within you, hoping it'll go away. Or, try to silence it with the noise of the many distractions this life offers you. But, of course, to no avail. Maybe that's you. Maybe you are a Christian who has gone to church for years but has never really understood who God is, as it relates to you, or who you are as it relates to Him. Do you want to understand more about your heavenly heritage? Are you fed up with doing the religious thing, but not experiencing the real thing? Are you ready to take your place in the company of *Anointed Lives Invading Every Nation Supernaturally*?

Well, if you are, then join me on this journey as we explore certain fundamentals of supernatural life you may have never known before. It is my prayer that as you thumb through these next few pages you will feel the rule and reign of God's Kingdom invading your heart and establishing His government in your life.

A.L.I.E.N.S.

CHAPTER 1
ONCE UPON A TIME

As a little boy, I loved the story of Superman. Like every other boy my age, I fantasized about flying through the sky, seeing through walls, and being stronger than any mortal man. I felt like I related to him. Not the superhero, so much. I related to the awkward teenage boy on a quest to find out where he came from. I enjoyed drinking a hot chocolate and watching black and white country and Western movies with my father every now and again. But my favorite version of Superman was not the 1952 black and white television series, *The Adventures of Superman*, it was the 1978 smash hit movie, *Superman*, starring Christopher Reeves.

I was only two years old when it came out in the movie theaters, and I watched it on television when I was about six years old. My three-year obsession with Spiderman, Batman, and the Incredible Hulk was brought to a screeching halt when the orphaned alien from Krypton swooped down into my world and filled my active imagination with endless possibilities. I was so obsessed with him, in fact, that my older sister Trudy loves to remind me of how I once wore a Superman outfit to school in the third grade. That's right. I wore a Superman outfit to school, cape and all—and it wasn't even Halloween, an event I vaguely remember, and I plan to keep it that way.

Why my parents allowed me to do this, I do not know, but my wife thinks it makes for good laughs today. And so do I, but I won't let her know that. I was fascinated with the phenomenal feats Superman would accomplish, and imagined myself doing the same. Effortlessly flying through the sky, preventing world catastrophes, seeing through walls, and bringing evil villains to their knees.

But as I got older, it was the story of Superman that intrigued me. Not so much the story of the full-grown superhero, but of a teenage Clark Kent, who knew he was from another world far, far away, and would never quite fit in here. I felt the heartache of the boy on the road to self-discovery. I felt silly for understanding him, but I did understand him. I identified with the loneliness he seemed to feel as he watched his schoolmates play football, go out with pretty girls, and revel in the blissful ignorance of normalcy.

I thought about my friends, and how unaware they seemed to be of the world around them. It bothered me that they were never bothered by the things that bothered me. I was raised in a Christian home, but I wasn't a Christian yet. "So, what makes me so different?" I thought. "Why does it feel like I've been chosen to carry a burden I never asked for? Why doesn't getting drunk, smoking cigarettes, and cursing like a sailor get rid of this longing within me. Why can't I seem to drown out this inaudible voice that keeps calling me? Why do I feel like this? As if I lost something I used to have. As if someone is deliberately orchestrating the events of my life to guide me back to it."

My favorite part of the movie is when Clark finds what's left of the planet Krypton, his birthplace, and views the prerecorded messages his father, Jor-El left for him. He sees his father for the first time and discovers who he really is. He's not Clark Kent, the earthling. He's Kal-El, the Kryptonian. His father sent him to Earth to use his powers to accomplish extraordinary things. He finally understood what the longing within him was all about.

It wasn't to outrun trains, leap tall buildings, and fly higher than all of the birds of the sky. It was for a purpose far greater than any of those things. It was to do good. He was powerful for a purpose that was greater than himself. It was a calling, and he would use his power to fulfill it. Something within me identified with that. I would soon learn why. The way I felt my entire life would make sense. I thought that if I became popular and started going out with pretty girls I would feel differently. But at 14, I was fairly popular. I was the class clown, and well-liked by various pretty girls. But I still felt the same inside - lost and alone.

Like Clark Kent, the continuous longing I felt was a calling. It was the call of God fidgeting within me like a restless toddler in the waiting room of a doctor's office. It was making me uncomfortable, and dissatisfied with anything other than the only environment that would ignite it. The environment of God's presence!

The eternity that God had planted in my heart before I was born was constantly tugging at my sensibilities. I wanted to know what I was born for, but I had to first find out where I came from. Not my earthly origin, but my heavenly origin. I needed to discover my once-upon-a-time so that I could live my happily-ever-after. It was the same thing that happened to Clark Kent. Or so I would imagine the untold fictional story in my mind's eye. It would read somewhat like this:

His parents had done the very best they could. They raised him like he was their very own flesh and blood for fourteen years. Now, fast approaching his 15th birthday, Clark seemed to become more somber and withdrawn. His gaze was pensive, and his words were fewer day by day. Almost as if he was listening for someone or something.

His presence was increasingly otherworldly. A big part of him just wanted to fit in with everybody else, while an even bigger part of him wanted to show everyone the spectacular things that he was discovering about himself every day. He wanted everyone to know the real him. Not this watered-down version of himself that was acceptable to society.

Mrs. Kent knew that no matter how many times she pleaded with Clark to suppress his supernatural identity, he couldn't keep burying the desire within him to outrun trains, leap tall buildings, and look through walls. He couldn't help it. It's what he was born to do.

The only thing that she could do for him, as his mother, was knit him a sweater, cook him a hot meal, and tell him how much she loved him. All his dad could do was tell him about the birds and the bees, watch the game with him on TV, and ask him how his day went.

Clark had great parents. In fact, he had the kind of parents that every child should have. But no matter how great they were, they could never answer the questions in his mind or fill the enormous void in his heart. He was not from this world, so nothing and no one in this world could help him understand who he really was.

Clark found out why he was sent when he encountered the one who had sent him. That's how it works. That's how God introduces Himself to us. By putting things around us that agitate the purpose He placed within us. You might ask, what kind of things does God put around us? Well, everything, actually. Our family, friends, and even our experiences. Experiences like not fitting in, being rejected by people you admire, and even excelling at things that give you no satisfaction.

I have given pastoral counsel to numerous people who have graduated at the top of their class, got the job they always wanted, and married the person of their dreams. But they confess that they still feel like they've not begun to live. Not until you discover your heavenly origin, in the presence of the one who sent you to the Earth, will that change. When you encounter the one who sent you into the world, that's when you'll understand the reason why you were sent.

It wouldn't be until years later that I would understand the spiritual principles I saw in that movie and others like it. As to whether or not the creator of Superman intended some spiritual parallel to be derived from his adventures, I don't know. It's probably unlikely. Even though I didn't yet understand it, I certainly felt it. Maybe I was the only one.

But this fictional story rang true for me. For my peers, on the other hand, it was nothing more than a fairy tale for every boy under the age of 12 to daydream about. But to me, it applied to everyone. Even those who didn't realize it yet. Not just Superman, but even the bedtime stories parents read to their children at night before they tucked them in. There's a reason why those fairy tales begin with "Once upon a time . . ." and end with ". . . they lived happily ever after." It's not just because we want our children to get a good night's sleep with visions of grandeur dancing in their heads.

It's because long ago, in a land far, far away, you and I came from "Once upon a time," where the Lord of Heaven made us for "Happily ever after." Our sci-fi, *Marvel* comics, and fairy tale storybooks are not just the result of creative authors with overactive imaginations. I believe it's because, subconsciously, we remember where we come from. Our human spirit remembers. We remember once upon a time. And our sinful state is the spiritual amnesia that has stolen our happily ever after.

Jensen Franklin, the Senior Pastor of Free Chapel Worship Center in Gainesville, Georgia, told a story that brought tears to my wife's eyes as she eagerly shared it with me. It's about a little boy who couldn't wait for his new baby sister to come home from the hospital. He couldn't wait to be near her so he could talk to her. But his parents didn't want him to be left alone with her yet because he was only four years old. Too young to understand the kind of care a newborn needs.

They wanted to supervise his time with her. He kept begging to be alone with her, so one night, his parents finally let him get the time with her he was asking for. The boy walked into his baby sister's room, stood next to her crib, and said: "Hurry up and tell me about God. I'm starting to forget." What an adorable yet profound story. This is the reason why God placed a desire for eternity in our hearts. Because He knows that our spiritual amnesia, resulting from the curse of sin, has caused the human race to forget what we once were. And only our longing for *happily ever after* would cause us to desperately search for *once upon a time*.

Remembering

When we fantasize about a world with endless possibilities and portals that lead to magical lands filled with love, peace, and exhilarating adventures, we think we're only imagining, but we're actually remembering. I do not necessarily mean that we remember specific events as they actually transpired a long time ago. But we subconsciously remember the limitless possibilities of a life without carnal constraints.

Just as you would drive down a street you don't recall ever driving on before, but everything about it seems eerily familiar to you. You even anticipate what you'll see next, and sure enough, there it is. But it's not so much what you see on that street that momentarily bewilders you. It's that rather strange, "I was here before" feeling. We've all felt it at some time or another. You don't know why or how. But something just feels oddly familiar. "Why do I feel like I know this place, yet I know nothing about this place?"

The French refer to it as déjà vu. It means "already seen." Have you ever wondered why that happens to you? Why you occasionally feel as if you're remembering something that never happened before? It seems absurd, doesn't it? I have often wondered about this. "Am I remembering something, or is this a glitch in the matrix of my brain?" Whatever déjà vu actually is, I believe it speaks to the larger truth, that something within us remembers what we were before we became what we are now. We are sinful beings, separated from the source of our identity, God, the Creator.

I don't believe in reincarnation. The Bible tells us that it's appointed to everyone to die at least once, and after this, the judgment. But I do believe that every human spirit has flashbacks of Once Upon a Time. So that's why some things that have never happened before seem so familiar to us. It's because, somehow, the eternal part of us has already seen it. Especially when we get in the Presence of God. Even prayer seems familiar to those who've never prayed. Because prayer creates a portal into God's Presence, and our eternal identity remembers the environment in which it was designed.

Ephesians 1:4 NIV

"For he chose us in Him before the creation of the world to be holy and blameless in his sight. In love."

If we were in God before the creation of the world, then we existed before the world was created. That means that we are as timeless as God is. That's what we remember! We remember God! God is our once upon a time, and our happily ever after. He is omnipresent. Not just in all of space but also in all of time. He exists in all places, realms, and dimensions at once. He lives in all of time, at all times. God is currently present in the past, in the present, and in the future. He does not have a past or a future. He only has a present. That's why He rejoices about your future because He not only knows what's coming, He's already there. Think about that! God is in your future, and you are in God, and God is in you. That'll keep you up at night.

So, when you pray in the present, God receives it because He is living in your today. Then He goes back to your past and wipes your slate clean because He is living in your yesterday. Then He goes to your future and applies your prayer to your destiny, creating a brand-new life for you, because He is living in your tomorrow. He goes into your yesterday and forgives you of everything you've ever done. Then he goes into your tomorrow and changes the destiny you would have had had you never prayed.

Then He comes back to you today, and gives you hope for the brand new future you inherited in Him when you prayed. And the miracle is, He did all of this at the same time because He exists in all of time, at all times! I don't know if this accounts for déjà vu, but it certainly accounts for the familiar feeling we have when we're in God's Presence.

When I was 14 years old, in the ninth grade, I was no longer running around the hallways of my school in a Superman suit. Nor did I want to, thank God. But I still wanted to feel what watching movies like that made me feel like a child. I still sensed a longing within me for once upon a time and happily ever after. When I came to God at 15 years old, I felt every bit of that happily ever after. It was far more exciting and thrilling than any superhero movie I had ever watched before.

I felt like fire was burning away my addictions to cigarettes, marijuana, and alcohol. I felt my thoughts changing. It was as if electricity was surging through my physical body. I knew I was feeling the power of God. This experience surpassed anything I could have ever imagined. It was as if I was inhaling and exhaling for the first time. I knew I was created for this! It was as if the ceiling between Heaven and Earth was pulled back, and with wide-eyed wonder, I gazed at the world with brand new eyes. One Sunday morning in a little church on the outskirts of Baltimore, Maryland, my spiritual amnesia was cured. I encountered my Heavenly Father, and I remembered who He was, who I was, and where I came from.

WHEN THE KINGDOM OF GOD IS PRESENT, IT DOESN'T RELINQUISH ANYTHING TO THE KINGDOM OF DARKNESS.

A.L.I.E.N.S.

CHAPTER 2
THE INVASION BEGINS

Perhaps it was the many late-night conversations in my father's car in the spring of 1992. Maybe that's where it started? My fascination with the concept of Heaven, that is. I was 15 years old, a brand-new Christian, and deeply passionate about my relationship with God. By this time, my mom and dad had been divorced for at least three years. My father worked for BWI airport, delivering lost luggage, and would pick me up to accompany him on some of his deliveries.

No matter what our conversations were for the first 30 or so minutes, it always came back to the one topic we both loved the most—God! His person, presence, and purposes. Oh sure, we'd start off talking about how school was, how work was, and how my sisters, Trudy and Latoya, were doing. We'd discuss history and political events. But we both knew where the conversation would eventually end up. Even the weightiest of topics were to us like feathers in a windstorm. The feathers were all of the trite and trivial matters of life, and the windstorm was God. How I longed every moment of those days to be carried away by the windstorm of His presence.

Nearing the end of his route, my father would take me back home, off Liberty Road, to Shakespeare Park Apartments in Randallstown, Maryland. A two-bedroom apartment I shared with my mother and two sisters. My father would pull into one of the parking spaces in front of my apartment building, and we would sit there for, at the very least, two to three hours.

It was as if all we had discussed so far was merely the precursor to the real thing. The appetizer before the main course. And what a main course it was to be! I remember being transfixed by his thick Jamaican accent and deep bellowing voice detailing the various heavenly encounters and angelic visitations he had in his youth. These were not fancy-filled fictional stories he was making up. The truth of his words oozed through his pores!

Heaven was not just a place he read about in the Bible. It was a place he had been! And from the look in his eyes, it was quite possibly a place he never left. These conversations induced an appetite within me to not only experience these things for myself but to understand why it now seemed second nature to me to crave these experiences. You see, it wasn't my father's stories that caused me to seek to have an encounter with God. It was actually a life-altering encounter with God that caused me to inquire about my father's stories.

We were like drinking buddies on a stoop, sharing the same flask and exchanging tales too fantastic to believe, unless you, too, were drinking out of the same flask. When I would leave my father's car and go upstairs to the second floor, where my mother and sisters were watching TV, doing their hair, or having dinner, I would give them a polite yet aloof greeting. Hoping no one would attempt to engage me in a conversation that would keep me from the urgent task before me. The task of getting into my bedroom as quickly as possible.

For many days and nights before this one, every time I closed the door to my bedroom, and was alone on the other side, it would immediately become God's throne room, and I would collapse at His feet! Anxious for the glorious experience awaiting me across the threshold of my bedroom door, I walked with the urgency of a man who needed to get to the bathroom before his bladder exploded.

"Rohan, what's wrong?" My mother would ask. Concerned, her only son seemed deeply troubled. "Nothing's wrong with him, Mommy." My little sister, Latoya, would calmly say. "He's just going to pray." Not that my mother was any stranger to the desire to be in God's presence. She received her share of close encounters with the Lord. I remember being awakened on various occasions by her crying out to God in the middle of the living room floor, "Oh God, keep my children in your arms. Protect them, cover them, and give them the heart to serve you!" Wrapped in a white bed sheet, I remember her praying as if her very life depended on it.

But this was not her crying out to God this time. It was me, her 15-year-old son. Overnight, my entire life had experienced a 180- degree turn. I was no longer roaming the streets or getting into trouble. All of which she was grateful for. But perhaps my newfound faith seemed a bit extreme. For months, I lost my appetite for food, friends, watching television, or even casual conversations. I didn't read a portion of Scripture that necessarily dissuaded me from any of these things. Nor did my Pastor preach sermons against watching television, going out with friends, or normal, everyday chit-chat.

I felt about these things the same way I felt about the girl I broke up with in the fifth grade. She was the most popular girl in my school, and everyone thought I was so lucky she wanted to hang out with me. So did I at first. But after calling her my girlfriend for one week, I simply lost interest. My seemingly fanatical behavior was not because I had become indoctrinated. I was not a legalist about the things of God. I had just become a lover of God. I was obsessed with God and everything about Him. I was equally repulsed by anything that detracted from my ability to create an environment for the things I was experiencing. I know that might sound super religious to some, but to me, it was quite the opposite. It was utopian, and I was in love. Those who cared about me were glad that I had changed. It was obvious that I had changed for the better. But they were concerned that maybe I was changing a bit too drastically.

For me, however, the transformation was not nearly drastic enough. These experiences beyond the threshold of my bedroom door and late-night conversations in my father's car had caused me to realize just how far the church had backslidden. We were no longer heavenly-minded. We were all together, earthly-minded. Our interests, conversations, so-called worship songs, and even our sermons, "All earthly!" Our carnality was a thief that had robbed us of the joys of Heaven, our native land.

I became obsessed and even addicted to being in the presence of God! I didn't know that I had a prayer life. To me, it didn't feel like I was praying. It just felt like I was breathing. And the times I spent watching TV or just hanging out with people felt like I was just holding my breath until I could gasp for air again. I felt that if I didn't spend all the time I could with God, I would die. My Spirit was communicating with God's Spirit, and my desires were being transformed. My life as an unbeliever was extreme, so my new life as a believer had to be extreme as well.

The English Evangelist and biblical scholar A.W. Pink said, "Real prayer is communion with God so that there will be common thoughts between His mind and ours. What is needed is for Him to fill our hearts with His thoughts, and then His desires will become our desires flowing back to Him."

I didn't know about A.W. Pink back then, but I love that definition of prayer. And that's exactly what was happening to me. My desires became God's desires flowing back to Him. And I lived the rest of my teenage years in hot pursuit of that exchange.

Chasing the Moon

The thing my father said to me the most was, "Keep your eyes on Jesus." It's the best advice I've ever received. I didn't know this then, but following that advice would be like chasing the moon. A few years ago, my cousin Claudine and her husband Vaughn bought a telescope. I was as giddy as a child with excitement and anticipation to go over to their house and play with their new toy. I've always loved the beauty and mystery of outer space. I believe that humans were created to have telescopic vision. I also believe we lost this ability when man fell from his righteous state. So, I've always been fascinated with the ability to see into space.

Vaughn and I went outside on his porch, and he was showing me how to use the telescope. We located the moon, and it was truly amazing to see it up close and personal. The telescope came with a remote attachment that we used to keep track of the Moon. Because the Moon is orbiting around the Earth, it's constantly moving. And because the Earth orbits the Sun, it is also constantly moving. Because of this, I had to keep using the arrows on the remote, down, up, left, and right, to keep the Moon in view.

While we were out there, a thought came to me. I realized that because we, on Earth, were moving away from what we were seeing, and the Moon was also moving away from us, we had to keep making adjustments in order to keep it in view. This principle is also true of spiritual things. Because we, in our earthly, sinful condition, are constantly moving away from our revelation and vision of God, we have to be deliberate about constantly making adjustments to keep our revelation of Him in view. God is also constantly moving, so in order to sustain a vision of Him, we must continuously move toward Him. That's how we keep our eyes on Jesus.

Hebrews 12:1-2 NIV

...since we are surrounded by such a great cloud of witnesses, let us throw off everything that hinders and the sin that so easily entangles. And let us run with perseverance the race marked out for us, fixing our eyes on Jesus, the pioneer and perfecter of faith...

Just as I had to keep pushing the arrows to move the telescope in different directions, so must we keep making ongoing adjustments in our daily walk with God to keep up with our progressive revelation of who He is. Years ago, Tommy Tinny wrote a book called *God Chasers* that reminded the Church of how important it is to passionately pursue God. Something we need to be reminded of constantly.

I really enjoyed seeing the Moon, but when I paused too long to enjoy the view, it would begin to escape my vision. It was as if I had to keep chasing the Moon in order to keep viewing it in real-time. And so it is with Spiritual things. If you want to keep a fresh vision of God before you, you have to keep chasing Him. It's the reasonable price you have to pay to behold heavenly things.

The Moon never stood still for me to see it conveniently, and God does not stand still for us to see Him conveniently. The pursuit of Him is an adventure! I didn't have to chase Him for salvation, but I do have to chase Him to sustain a revelation of the one who saved me.

The Moon is available every night for everyone to see. You don't have to get a telescope and chase it to see it from a distance. Just open your eyes, look out your bedroom window, and it'll be there. But if you want to see it up-close, in real-time, from planet Earth, you're going to have to learn how to use a telescope and chase it.

God's majesty and magnificence are available all the time for everyone to see. All you have to do is open your eyes and look around you. It's there! But if you want to see God, I mean really see Him, up close and personal, it's not going to be as simple and convenient as opening your eyes and looking around you. It's going to be as deliberate, adventurous, and inconvenient as chasing the Moon.

Where God Is, Where I Am

At 15 years old, an appetite had been induced within me that would become my lifelong mission. You see, I didn't just develop a fascination with Heaven. I developed a fascination with the concept of Heaven. The concept of Heaven, to my 15-year-old poetic mind was this, "God likes to hang out there because He created it to be the most suitable and adequate environment to host His presence."

Wow! What a thought! I knew I was on to something. But it wouldn't be until a few months later that I would follow that thought to its logical conclusion and connect the dots. One day, I was reading the gospels, and I came across Jesus teaching His disciples how to pray. A prayer most everyone, Christians and non-Christians alike, are familiar with.

"Our Father who art in Heaven...Thy Kingdom Come. Thy will be done on Earth as it is in Heaven." For the very first time, I realized something about prayer I had never known before. "It starts out talking about where God is, and ends up talking about where I am." The prayer starts out in Heaven, where God is, and ends up on the Earth, where I am. "That's it! That's what prayer is! That's what's been happening to me!" I wanted to open my bedroom window and shout it so the whole neighborhood could hear me. "If you get a revelation of what's going on where He is, then it will change what's going on where you are!!"

This was the first of many revolutionary concepts God would show me from the scriptures. I was now able to connect the dots.

Matthew 6:9-13

"So then if Heaven is the most suitable and adequate environment for God's presence and Jesus tells us to pray, Your Kingdom come, Your will be done

on Earth as it is in Heaven. Maybe God's greatest desire is not only for us to be where He is, but for us to also create an environment that is so similar to where He is, that it makes it possible for Him to be where we are.

Over 30 years later, this is still very much my obsession. With every sermon I preach, every Bible study I teach, and every person I council. This is my prayer. That every action of obedience I give to God will become a doorway and a portal through which His Kingdom can come, and His will can be done on Earth as it is in Heaven.

At 15 years old, my prayers didn't sound quite this theological. I wasn't talking to God about portals from heavenly dimensions into earthly realms. But with my face buried in the carpet and my uncontrollable sobbing, only to be interrupted by guttural whispers of praise, I had become a portal from Heaven to Earth. Heaven was not an abstract concept to me. It was closer to me than my bedroom ceiling. I felt it descending upon me! I became addicted to prayer because I was addicted to experiencing the presence of God.

Kingdoms Don't Co-Exist

At my invitation, God's Kingdom invaded my heart. And I soon learned that invading kingdoms don't know how to co-exist with the Kingdom that is currently ruling the territory they've invaded. The Kingdom of Jesus Christ was not content to co-exist with the kingdom of Rohan Peart. When He came into my heart, He completely overthrew my other affections and took over my life.

When the military legend and genius Alexander the Great invaded a ruling kingdom, it was obvious to the defending inhabitants that their country had been invaded. When he conquered Egypt, he overthrew the Persian administration that was governing it at the time. He then founded a city in Egypt and named it after himself. Alexandria, Egypt. There was no mistaking who was in charge. That's how Kings rule.

Jesus is the King of all Kings, but most Christians don't treat Him that way because they don't view Him that way. So many Christians view God as a lovable, quiet grandfather who doesn't ever intrude on their personal affairs or get involved in the complicated aspects of their lives.

He's just there whenever they need a shoulder to cry on or advice from someone wiser than themselves. But that's not who God is at all. God is not the strong, silent type who only gets involved when there's a crisis or when you're willing to think about considering His advice.

King Jesus doesn't come into your life to become a part of it. He comes into your life to give you His life and make you a part of His Kingdom. He's not the Man in the sky that you acknowledge at weddings, funerals, and baby christenings. He's not a warm fuzzy teddy bear that you pick up and put down when you feel like it. In fact, you don't decide where you're going to put Him in your world; He decides where He puts you in His Kingdom. Kings don't go where people put them; kings only go where people please them. As citizens of God's Kingdom, we don't get to add the King to our life. We only get to acknowledge that the King is our life. And when we do that, the King will give us the most adventurous life that will exceed our wildest expectations.

Evidence of Invasion

Wherever a king goes, the glory, majesty, and authority of his kingdom goes with him. He can't hide it and wouldn't even if he could. Wherever God goes, the glory, majesty, and authority of His Kingdom goes with Him. So, if you are a believer in Jesus Christ (washed in His blood and born of His Spirit), then that means the glory, majesty, and authority of the Kingdom of God has taken over your life! And if that has happened, such a thing will be obvious to you and everyone who knows you. If it's not obvious to you and those who know you, then it probably hasn't happened.

When a kingdom invades the territory of another kingdom, it doesn't happen quietly and without conflict. There are horses, foot soldiers, battleships, planes, tanks, fighter jets, blood, sweat, tears, and an overabundance of weaponry. It's not quiet, and it's not cheap. It's expensive, and if you're on the winning side, it's economically profitable.

When God's Kingdom invades the spiritual territory of the darkened hearts of men, it doesn't happen quietly. The man it has happened to may not jump up and down for joy, but every addiction, attitude, and mindset that is inconsistent with the government of God will be confronted by the word and ways of the King. And without Him even trying, everyone who knows Him will know that something drastic has happened to Him.

Luke 11:20-22, NLT

But if I am casting out demons by the power of God, then the Kingdom of God has arrived among you.[21] For when a strong man like Satan is fully armed and guards his palace, his possessions are safe—[22] until someone even stronger attacks and overpowers him, strips him of his weapons, and carries off his belongings.

Jesus' point is that supernatural activity is the evidence that the Kingdom of God has invaded the world. If there is no supernatural activity, the Kingdom of God is not present. It's that simple. Because wherever the Kingdom goes, God's word and ways manifest His Presence and power. Jesus is saying, "The way that you can know the Kingdom of God has arrived is when someone who is a part of it starts demonstrating the supernatural power of God!

Jesus was casting out demons because demons are a part of the hierarchy of the government of Satan. Jesus was overthrowing the Satanic government in order to establish His own government on Earth. But the reason He was publicly casting out demons is because He was making an announcement. That announcement was, "An invasion is taking place!" The supernatural is a demonstration of the military might of God's Kingdom. Supernatural activity, in the name of the King, is the sign of Divine invasion. The lack thereof is a sign that the Kingdom of God is not present.

When the Kingdom of God arrives on Earth, according to Jesus several things will happen:

1. The Kingdom of God will be stronger than the Kingdom of darkness.

    - *When the Kingdom of God is present, it is always the dominating force on Earth.*

2. Those from the Kingdom of Light will attack and overpower the Kingdom of Darkness.

- *When the Kingdom of God is present, it's not on the defense; it's on the offense.*

3. Those from the Kingdom of Light will strip the kingdom of darkness of its weapons.

    - *When the Kingdom comes, there will be an evident shift in the influence of power and authority.*

4. Those from the Kingdom of Light will take away the things that previously belonged to the Kingdom of Darkness.

    - *When the Kingdom of God is present, it doesn't relinquish anything to the Kingdom of Darkness. It restores and recovers all resources.*

I like to say it this way, "Devil, you can't have nothin'!!" I know that's grammatically incorrect, but it just feels good to say it that way! "You can't have my mind, my marriage, my children, or my money, because the King of the Kingdom I belong to has commanded me to restore and recover it all!!" Stop reading for a moment, take 30 seconds and praise God that the Kingdom of Light is stronger than the Kingdom of Darkness. Hallelujah!!! Thank you, Lord!!

We Need an Invasion

Every so often, probably more than we know, UFO sightings are reported. People are fascinated with them because they mark the unknown. For most of us on this planet, ordinary everyday lives have never been interrupted because of UFO sightings. Unidentified flying objects, occasionally seen from a distance, to my knowledge have never been a real concern to any nation's national security, or our global safety. Even though three former military officials told Congress in the summer of 2023 that they believe the government knows much more about UFOs than it is telling the public.

A House Oversight subcommittee held a hearing on UFOs, officially known as unidentified aerial phenomena or UAPs—and heard shocking testimony about unexplained object sightings and government possession of "nonhuman" biological matter. So, even though there is some validity to the chatter of aliens from outer space possibly existing, to my knowledge, there is currently no imminent threat of an alien invasion. But if aircraft from outer space start landing in major cities of the world, descending on highways in the middle of rush hour traffic, without knowing who or what they are, panic will ensue all over the planet.

In the famous 1997 movie *Independence Day*, starring Will Smith, there was a terrifying worldwide alien invasion. The movie depicted the American government receiving some sort of communication from outer space. They kept a close eye on it but were not alarmed until they realized the UFOs had entered Earth's atmosphere without the authorization to do so. Soon, widespread pandemonium broke out.

In every alien movie that I've seen, as long as the UFOs keep their distance, everyone is curious, intrigued, and even fascinated. But when the spaceships land, everybody goes crazy. And it's the same way with those of us whom God has sent into the world to establish His Kingdom in people's hearts. As long as we keep our distance, mind our own business, and go to church on Sunday, no one minds if, every now and again, a random miracle occurs among us. But if it starts to happen too frequently and too close to home, then the power of God becomes a threat. We need to stop our UFO (doing the God thing from a distance) and non-threatening Christianity, and we need an invasion of the supernatural power of God in the world today! We need to stop being the safe Goody Two-Shoes and start being the dangerous good Samaritans, whose acts of righteousness threaten the enemy's kingdom.

In any alien movie you watch, you'll see the same thing. The moment that random occasional UFO sightings become verifiable undeniable spaceship landings, four things became terribly obvious to the residents of the world.

1. An unearthly society of supernatural beings has invaded the Earth.

2. They have come to take over.

3. We must prepare to surrender to them or wage war against them.

4. Our world as we have known it has come to an end.

When the random occurrences of miraculous activity and Christ-like conduct that is occasionally sighted in our churches workplaces, schools, and communities become the norm, visibly impacting every arena of the world, it will become glaringly evident to everyone that those who are called Christians are:

1. An unearthly society of people with supernatural abilities, whose heavenly mothership has invaded the world system.

2. These believers are a part of a heavenly Kingdom that has come to take over.

3. The inhabitants of the Earth must prepare to surrender to this Kingdom, or wage war against it.

4. The world as they knew it had come to an end.

These are the things that non-Christians thought when they saw the activities of the early Church. They were threatened by them! These were men and women performing miracles, talking about a Kingdom from another world, and converting people to that Kingdom with love instead of hate. A spiritual revolution was having a religious, social, moral, and political impact that changed the world as they knew it. And by political impact, I don't mean that the church became political. I rather mean that even the political officials took notice because the church's influence began to shift the culture.

Acts 17:5-6 NKJV

But the Jews who were not persuaded, becoming envious, took some of the evil men from the marketplace and gathering a mob, set all the city in an uproar and attacked the house of Jason and sought to bring them out to the people. But when they did not find them, they dragged Jason and some brethren to the rulers of the city, crying out, "These who have turned the world upside down have come here too."

When a Christian family moves into a community or a Church is being planted in a new location, the people of the community ought to notice a difference. They shouldn't be indifferent and completely comfortable living in the same community as believers. There should be something about us that stirs them up. Not our arrogance and know-it-all, combative, self-righteous attitudes. No! There ought to be a fire ignited within them because of how passionate we are about God's love for them. We shouldn't just blend in! Because kingdoms don't co-exist, they take over! So when they see us coming, they ought to say to one another, "Those who have turned the world upside down have come here too."

At 15 years old, it was evident to my friends that something dramatic had taken place in my life. I started a Bible study at my school and led many of my classmates to Christ. I cried for one whole year after I came to faith in Jesus Christ. One entire year of nonstop weeping. I wasn't weeping because of sadness, but gratefulness. Every single day for at least a year, I collapsed at the feet of my Savior, overcome with euphoria and anguish! Sometimes, the tears would flow all day long. Can you imagine that? I couldn't even pray over a meal without bursting into tears. It should have been embarrassing to me, but I wasn't the least bit embarrassed. I actually felt sorry for people who didn't feel what I was feeling. The love, joy, and sorrow of the Lord constantly flooded my heart.

At my Church, they called me Jeremiah, the weeping Prophet. People thought I was out of my mind. But miracles were happening all around me. God began to tell me things about people that blew their minds and mine as well. I prayed for people to be healed, and they were physically healed. I knew things about people I couldn't possibly know unless the Lord had revealed them to me. Sometimes, I didn't even realize I was prophesying. There were times when I would be having what I thought was a normal conversation, and the person I was talking to would stop me and say, "How did you know that?" And I would say, "How did I know what?" I prophesied to them without even realizing it.

It was evident that the Kingdom of God had invaded my life. He was turning my world, and the worlds of those who knew me, upside down. The heavenly mothership had landed in my bedroom. And the world as I knew it had come to an end. It all started with the agonizing request of a 15-year-old boy, pleading with God in his bedroom. For hours, I would chant, "Your kingdom come. Your Kingdom come. Your Kingdom come." I didn't understand the implications of my invitation or the ramifications of my request. I only knew that the world I had known my entire life would one day be invaded by the world I was just introduced to. I also knew that I didn't need to wait for that invasion. But that somehow, it could start right now, and right here, in this room, with me.

CHAPTER 3
NOT OF THIS WORLD

John 18:33-37 NLT

³³Then Pilate went back into his headquarters and called for Jesus to be brought to him. "Are you the king of the Jews?" he asked him. ³⁴ Jesus replied, "Is this your own question, or did others tell you about me?" ³⁵ "Am I a Jew?" Pilate retorted. "Your own people and their leading priests brought you to me for trial. Why? What have you done?" ³⁶ Jesus answered, "My Kingdom is not an earthly kingdom. If it were, my followers would fight to keep me from being handed over to the Jewish leaders. But my Kingdom is not of this world." ³⁷ Pilate said, "So you are a king?" Jesus responded, "You say I am a king. Actually, I was born and came into the world to testify to the truth. All who love the truth recognize that what I say is true."

What's an Alien?

There are several definitions of the word alien. An alien can be a foreigner who is not a naturalized citizen of the country in which they are living. Or they can be a resident, born in or belonging to another country. An alien can also be a being from another world. Those of us who are believers in Jesus Christ are aliens. We are beings from another world, born in and belonging to another society. That society is the Kingdom of Heaven. Though we are physically born on Earth, we are not citizens of the world system that is governed by the Kingdom of Darkness. We are citizens of the Kingdom of God if we, by the Spirit of God, are born into it.

Philippians 3:20-21, NLT

But we are citizens of Heaven, where the Lord Jesus Christ lives. And we are eagerly waiting for Him to return as our Savior. [21] He will take our weak mortal bodies and change them into glorious bodies like His own, using the same power with which He will bring everything under His control.

When we pray for the Kingdom of God to come into the world, we're really praying for an alien invasion. We're praying for every life that has been awakened and anointed by God's Holy Spirit to invade every nation with the supernatural power to establish His Kingdom.

NOT OF THIS WORLD?

Those of us who grew up in the "old school" Pentecostal style of Church, where women wore no makeup or jewelry and sitting in a movie theater was equivalent to sitting on a barstool, have certain images that come to mind when we hear the phrase, "Not of this world."

My first recollection of hearing that phrase was when I was eight years old at the Red Door church in the city of Baltimore. The proper name of the church was actually Refuge Way of the Cross, but I don't remember anyone calling it that. They called it the Red Door Church. As a child, I thought that was actually the name of the church. I didn't realize that they only called it that because it had a big red door at the front of it. I was definitely not the sharpest tool in the shed.

Although I was only eight years old, I remember the power of God being evident in the sanctuary as the pastor would preach. In one particular service, they had a guest speaker. Although I was extremely young, I recall him preaching about Christians being different from the world. I don't remember if it was the subject of his entire sermon, but I do remember it standing out to me. He warned the congregation to stay away from the pleasures of sin and not to dress like the world, talk like the world, or act like the world.

Even as a child, I couldn't help but feel that, though all he was saying was true, there's got to be more to the story. He kept saying, "We are not of this world! We don't drink, curse, fornicate, smoke, cheat, lie or steal!"

Things along those lines.

Though I was grateful to hear about the world, we were not a part of, I kept thinking, "When is he going to start talking about the world we are a part of? God's world." I didn't know it then, but looking back, I realize that I wanted to hear him talk about the Kingdom of God.

To this day, I have a great deal of respect for that man of God and others like him. They paved the path for generations of preachers like myself to come behind them and pick up the mantle. They were serious about God, and though they didn't know a whole lot of Old Testament Hebrew or New Testament Greek, they knew how to pray, fast, and live consecrated lives before the Lord. But no matter how much we love and respect those who came before us, their model of ministry is not the standard for truth, nor is ours. God's Word is the standard for truth.

To be fair, I have the same issue with much of what I hear preached from our pulpits today. Probably even more so. This is not a problem that is specific to a particular generation. Every generation in real pursuit of God must overcome these hurdles. Before we go any further, let's identify the specific issue I'm referring to. There's a sense in which most of the things we teach about God are not altogether incorrect, but are still very much incomplete. Incomplete truth only becomes incorrect when it is taught as if it is the complete truth. For example, when we tell people to repent, we're correct in doing so. But if we present the message of repentance as if it's the whole message, then our incomplete message of repentance has just become incorrect.

John the Baptist and Jesus preached, "Repent for the Kingdom of Heaven is at hand." This was the correct message of repentance because it was the complete message of repentance. My only incentive to repent from something is that I am repenting for something. We've emphasized to the world the ugliness of the sin that they are repenting from instead of the beauty of the Kingdom that they are repenting for. The revelation of the King and His Kingdom is the reason for repentance! If we preach that, people will experience God's power and come to Him.

Romans 2:4 NKJV

...the goodness of God leads you to repentance...

When you realize how good he is in spite of how bad you are, it makes you want to turn away from all that is bad and put your trust in the only One that is good. The realization of how angry God is about my sin does not lead me to repentance. It's the realization of how good God is in spite of my sin that leads me to repent from it.

We have no right to call the world to repentance until we have demonstrated the power and glory of the Kingdom that is worthy of such a radical invitation.

I am not only responsible for preaching repentance in light of the Kingdom of God. I am also responsible for preaching repentance in light of my ability to demonstrate its power. That's why:

Romans 1:16 says, *"I am not ashamed of the gospel of Jesus Christ because it is the power of God unto salvation."* In other words, we SHOULD be ashamed of any gospel that lacks the ability to manifest the power of God's Kingdom. The word *gospel* means *good news*. When we tell the world, "Either repent or go to hell," with a hands-off, nonchalant attitude, that's not "good news." But when we tell others to repent and show them the glory of the Kingdom that is worthy of their repentance, they will plead, "What must we do to be saved?"

When Jesus told Pilate, "My Kingdom is not of this world," the word "world" used here is the Greek word kosmos. It means Political and social order. Jesus was admitting to Pilate that He was a King, and He did have a Kingdom. His admission communicated that the governmental and social structure of His kingdom was just as real as the Roman Empire's government was. But He was also stating that His Kingdom was different from, and superior to, the political and social order of the world system to which every Kingdom on Earth submits. He was confessing that He was an alien. He was an anointed life that had invaded the world for a purpose that the world did not yet understand. Pilot wasn't bothered by that because he did not see this spiritual Kingdom that Jesus was referring to as a threat to the Roman government. And that's pretty much all he cared about.

In this chapter, I want to focus on what it really means to not be of this world. What it means to be citizens of the Kingdom of Heaven.

Jesus' ability to undergo the ultimate persecution while in this world was because of the degree to which He understood the Kingdom He was a part of. Hebrews 12:2 says in the NLV, *"...He did not give up when He had to suffer shame and die on the cross. He knew of the joy that would be His later. Now He is sitting at the right side of God."*

By the same token, our ability to undergo all of the trials and tribulations we face while in this world will be because of the degree to which we understand the Kingdom we are a part of. The Kingdom of Heaven, to which we belong, is different than and superior to the kingdom of darkness that governs the political and the social order of the world system.

Hebrews 12:28-29 MSG

Do you see what we've got? An unshakable kingdom! And do you see how thankful we must be? Not only thankful, but brimming with worship, deeply reverent before God. For God is not an indifferent bystander. He's actively cleaning house, torching all that needs to burn, and He won't quit until it's all cleansed. God himself is Fire!

I love how the message Bible phrases this passage of Scripture.

"Do you see what we've got? An unshakable Kingdom! And do you see how thankful we must be? Not only thankful but brimming with worship, deeply reverent before God." If we really get a true vision of the unshakable Kingdom of God that we belong to; we will be thankful, reverent, and brimming with worship!"

Psalm 63:2-3 NLT

I have seen you in your sanctuary and gazed upon your power and glory. Your unfailing love is better than life itself; how I praise you!

If you have never been thankful, brimming with worship, and deeply reverent before God, I doubt very seriously that you have ever gazed upon the power and glory of the King who reigns over this unshakable Kingdom. We are not of this world! We are a part of a Kingdom that is not subject to the restrictions and limitations of this world system. Instead of fame, we seek to be known by God. Instead of money, we seek the eternal riches that reside in His glory. Instead of posturing for political power, we seek to be filled with the power of the Holy Spirit!

We're not of this world! But there's more to the story. We're no good to this world if we know that we don't belong to it, but we don't know about the world to which we belong. When this world system is shaking because of economic, political, and social unrest, the Kingdom we're a part of is not phased. The Kingdom of God only responds to the desires and decrees of the King. Nothing else. Likewise, the citizens of the Kingdom are not in the world to respond to the things that are going on in the world. We're in the world to respond to the desires and decrees of the one who put us here.

The reason most believers panic when bad things happen in the world is because they really don't understand that they are not subject to or governed by the spirit that is at work in the world around them. The bottom line is, they don't understand the Kingdom of God. Nor do they understand that they are citizens of the Kingdom of God. The passage of Scripture I probably quote the most while preaching and teaching is:

Proverbs 4:7... in all you're getting, get understanding.

I also like to say it this way: In all your getting, get understanding of all you're getting. Just because you have something doesn't necessarily mean it will be of any benefit to you. It only benefits you if you understand its function. And when you understand its function, that's when you attach value to it. Most citizens of the Kingdom of God have attached no value to God's Kingdom, because they don't understand how it functions or how they are supposed to function in it.

Ephesians 1:18-20 NLT

[18] I pray that your hearts will be flooded with light so that you can understand the confident hope He has given to those he called—His holy people who are His rich and glorious inheritance. [19] I also pray that you will understand the incredible greatness of God's power for those who believe Him. This is the same mighty power [20] that raised Christ from the dead and seated him in the place of honor at God's right hand in the heavenly realms.

Notice the language that Paul uses. He doesn't say I pray that you will receive, gain, or obtain the things that God has for you. He rather says, in essence, I pray that you will understand the things that God has given you. In other words, the church at Ephesus did not need God to give them anything; they just needed to understand what God had already given them.

This is my prayer for everyone who is a part of God's Kingdom. That we will really understand, from a biblical perspective, the protocol, practices, and principles of the Kingdom we're a part of.

Understanding the Kingdom

1 Corinthians 4:20 TLB

The Kingdom of God is not just talking; it is living by God's power.

The KJV says *it this way, "The Kingdom of God is not in word, but in power."*

The first thing I want to explain about the Kingdom of God is that it is a spiritual Kingdom. Not an imaginary Kingdom, a spiritual Kingdom. There is a big difference! Because it is a spiritual Kingdom, it must be spiritually discerned!

1 Corinthians 2:11-14 NLT

No one can know a person's thoughts except that person's own spirit, and no one can know God's thoughts except God's own Spirit. [12] And we have received God's Spirit (not the world's spirit), so we can know the wonderful things God has freely given us. [13] When we tell you these things, we do not use words that come from human wisdom. Instead, we speak words given to us by the Spirit, using the Spirit's words to explain spiritual truths. [14] But people who aren't spiritual can't receive these truths from God's Spirit. It all sounds foolish to them and they can't understand it, for only those who are spiritual can understand what the Spirit means.

The second thing I want to explain about the Kingdom of God is that no matter how much anyone explains it, it can never be sufficiently explained, it can only be experienced. In John Chapter 3, Jesus had a legendary conversation with a Pharisee and teacher of the law, named

Nicodemus. That conversation gave Nicodemus an education about the spiritual world that blew his mind, and revolutionized his understanding of the Kingdom of God.

John 3:1-8 NLT

There was a man named Nicodemus, a Jewish religious leader who was a Pharisee. ²After dark one evening, he came to speak with Jesus. ""Rabbi," he said, "we all know that God has sent you to teach us. Your miraculous signs are evidence that God is with you." ³Jesus replied, "I tell you the truth, unless you are born again, you cannot SEE the Kingdom of God." ⁴"What do you mean?" exclaimed Nicodemus. "How can an old man go back into his mother's womb and be born again?" ⁵ Jesus replied, "I assure you, no one can ENTER the Kingdom of God without being born of water and the Spirit. ⁶Humans can reproduce only human life, but the Holy Spirit gives birth to spiritual life. ⁷ So don't be surprised when I say, 'You must be born again.' ⁸ The wind blows wherever it wants. Just as you can hear the wind but can't tell where it comes from or where it is going, so you can't explain how people are born of the Spirit."

Most of us are so familiar with this passage that we don't realize that prior to Jesus, the Messiah, no one had ever spoken of the Kingdom of God in these terms. The reason Nicodemus was so confused is not because Jesus' statements were confusing. In fact Jesus seems a little taken aback by Nicodemus' bewilderment.

John 3:9-10 NLT

"How are these things possible?" Nicodemus asked. Jesus replied, ""You are a respected Jewish teacher, and yet you don't understand these things?"

Nicodemus, perhaps the most well-respected teacher of the word of God in that day, didn't understand the basic fundamentals of Spiritual living. Jesus reprimanded him for this. If the teacher doesn't understand, how will the students ever learn? This was not just enlightening for Nicodemus. I dare say it was probably enlightening for Jesus as well. As God, He knew all things, but as a Man he did not rely on the omniscience that was available to His divine nature. I believe that Jesus was enlightened in this exchange as to the level of spiritual ignorance in the religious establishment.

A parent may know that their 14-year-old child isn't good at ninth-grade math. Then, one day, while helping them with their homework, they realize that not only are they not good at ninth-grade math, they're horrible at the elementary school level of math as well. That's what I think happened here. Jesus' up close and personal conversation with Nicodemus caused him to wonder why Nicodemus was teaching when he clearly needed to be taught. A sentiment that would be expressed by the writer of the book of Hebrews several years later.

Hebrews 5:12 NLT

You have been believers so long now that you ought to be teaching others. Instead, you need someone to teach you the basic things about God's Word again. You are like babies who need milk and cannot eat solid food.

Today's breed of preachers suffers from the same ignorance as Nicodemus did. Very educated, articulate, and distinguished clergy who are well respected in their communities but in desperate need of an encounter with Jesus. For only a genuine encounter with Jesus, as Nicodemus had, will cure their spiritual ignorance, and open their eyes to the wonderful realities of the Kingdom of God. So, let's forget what we think we know about this passage in order to see it again with fresh eyes.

From Another World

It's important to note that the original manuscript does not say born again, as it is most often translated. The word translated "born again" is the Greek word anothen. It means "from above," and can also mean "of the Spirit." In essence, Jesus was saying unless a man be born of the Spirit in the world that is from above, he cannot see or enter the Kingdom of God.

Nicodemus was under the impression that all he had to do to see the Kingdom of God was to keep the law and wait for the Scriptures to be fulfilled. But Jesus informed him that unless he had the experience of being born into the Kingdom of God, he will never see, or enter into it. This concept was revolutionary to a man who had never thought about the Kingdom of God in such practical and literal terms. In Verse 6, Jesus gives him a course in biology as well as pneumatology. Pneumatology is the study of the Holy Spirit.

He says, "Humans can reproduce only human life, but the Holy Spirit gives birth to spiritual life."

The lesson that Jesus was teaching Nicodemus was this: "You are religious, but you are not spiritual. And until you allow the Holy Spirit to give you a spiritual birth, you will not be able to see or enter into the spiritual Kingdom of which I'm speaking." This is a vital truth that is not being taught in many of our churches today. It can be summed up like this. If you were never born of the spirit, it's impossible to live a spiritual life because you are not spiritually alive!

It always amazes me how preachers are so quick to tell the members of their churches who are facing issues of the flesh, "You just need to walk in the Spirit!" Making the assumption that the people they are speaking to have experienced a spiritual birth. This is a dangerous assumption! How can you require people to walk in a realm they've never been born in? How can I require you to be godly when you have never inherited God's nature?

That's both unfair and unreasonable. Yet that is the pressure we place on churchgoers all the time. There is pressure to do in the flesh what can only be done by the Spirit. It's interesting to me that as soon as Jesus starts talking to a religious teacher of the law about the Kingdom of God, He immediately emphasizes the necessity of spiritual birth. He doesn't talk to him about the Kingdom of God as it relates to good deeds and keeping the law. Why is that? I believe Jesus was sending a message to the religious establishment that Nicodemus represented.

Here is the message: I don't care how much of the Scriptures you think you understand and are able to teach, the Kingdom of God cannot be naturally explained; it must be spiritually experienced! That is what I believe Jesus was saying in a nutshell. In Verse 8, Jesus said, "The wind blows wherever it wants. Just as you can hear the wind but can't tell where it comes from or where it's going, so you can't explain how people are born of the Spirit."

This sums up everything Jesus was trying to tell Nicodemus all along. The process of spiritual birth is like the wind. You can feel and hear the wind. If it's powerful enough, you can even see its impact bending the strongest of trees and blowing the heaviest of debris. But no matter how much information you gather on the movement of the wind, you will never be able to sufficiently explain it, as well as you can experience it. No matter how much anyone explains the Kingdom of God, it can never be sufficiently explained; it can only be experienced.

How to Experience the Kingdom

The way to experience the Kingdom is to invite the rule and reign of the King to invade your heart and take over your life! We've all seen celebrities win awards and make acceptance speeches, where they thank God for the godless movie, song, or project that earned them their accolade. Or we've heard the rapper, country artist, or pop star whose lyrics promote sin and debauchery say things like, "I always put God first in my life."

I once saw an interview where a very well-known rap artist made that statement when asked why he was so successful, he said, "It's because I put God first." I cringed when I heard him say that. Not because I was unfairly judging him or believed him to be lying. But it was clear to me how sincere he was. He believed he was telling the truth. That frightened me! He didn't even know he lived a life and had beliefs that were contrary to the Scriptures.

By no means do I claim to have attained any level of perfection. I am as flawed as anyone else and probably more than most. My wife can attest to that. Hopefully, not too loudly though. My concern is not because I have unreasonable expectations of professing believers in Christ. It's because I have a very reasonable expectation of anyone who claims to know God. That is, they have invited the rule and reign of Jesus, the King, to invade their heart and take over their life.

The Kingdom of God is an actual society that is governed by God's laws. These laws are not rules that God suddenly decided to make up one day in an attempt to demonstrate how in charge He is. They are, as all laws of any society should be, a reflection of its values and of its vision.

The laws of God's Kingdom are a reflection of the principles of His divine nature. They create the framework for divine order. And that order creates an infrastructure that's able to house His presence, power, and purposes! The laws of the Kingdom are based on the ways and Word of the King.

One of those laws is, "In order to enter the Kingdom you have to be born of the spirit." Another way of saying that is, in order to gain access to the Kingdom you need to be related to the King. The only way to become related to the King is to repent. It's the Greek word *metanoia*. It means to change the way you think.

John and Jesus preached, "Repent for the Kingdom of Heaven is at hand." They didn't preach, join a synagogue or a church, be good to people, and give a lot of money to charity so that you can be a part of the Kingdom. They preached REPENTANCE. Metanoia! The only appropriate response to your revelation of the Kingdom is to allow it to invade every aspect of your life! And the only way that process begins is when you decide to exchange your way of thinking for God's way of thinking.

The difference between the believer and the unbeliever is not that the believer makes fewer mistakes than the unbeliever. Or the believer has stopped drinking, cursing, smoking, fornicating, and gambling. While the unbeliever continues to do all of these things. That's not it. The difference is simple. The believer has given the only appropriate response to the revelation of God's Kingdom. They have allowed it to invade every aspect of their life. They've decided to exchange their way of thinking for the King's way of thinking. They don't always cross every theological *T* and dot every ideological *I*. And they do mess up, as humans tend to do. But like the songwriter said, their eyes have seen the glory of the coming of the Lord! And they are ruined for anything else! There used to be a time when non-Christians knew they weren't Christians. They knew it didn't mean that God didn't love them or that they were less valuable than Christians. It just meant that they had not invited the King to invade their life with His Kingdom, and had not submitted to the process of exchanging their way of thinking for His way of thinking.

Nowadays, no matter what anyone believes or how they behave, they call themselves Christians. Truth is no longer being taught as *absolute*; it's being taught as whatever is relative to one's world view. So, people who have never been born of the Spirit are claiming citizenship in the Kingdom of God. It is already a challenging enough task to get people who know they need God to come to Him. Now, we have added to that challenge by watering down the messages we preach in so much that most people today believe that all it takes to be a Christian is going to church on a regular basis. But the Bible says, *"If any man be in Christ, he is a new creation. Old things are passed away, behold all things have become new."* (2 Corinthians 5:17)

It doesn't say if any man be in church, he is a new creation. There's a whole lot of people who are in church, who are not in Christ. Not because they're fakes, phonies, and hypocrites. I'm not referring to them. I'm referring to those who sincerely believe that they are a part of God's Kingdom, but they're really not. And the reason is because no one ever taught them how to become a part of it.

They were never taught that the only way to see and enter into the Kingdom of God is to be born into it. The term, born-again Christian, has become such a cliché that people think it's a religion or even a cult. They don't know that it is an experience given to you by the blood of Jesus washing away your sins and the Holy Spirit filling you with His life. This happens the moment you decide to give up your way of doing things in exchange for God's way of doing things. His love invades your heart, and takes over your life. That's how you are born into the Kingdom of God! The Kingdom that is not of this world.

Experiencing Spiritual Birth

Jesus was comparing spiritual birth to physical birth. The experience that a new babe in Christ has when they are born into God's Kingdom is comparable to the experience a baby has when they are born into the world. Just as a baby can feel the atmosphere, see and hear the environment, touch and taste the things in the world they've been born into, a person whose Spirit has just been born into the Kingdom of God can feel it, taste it, touch it, see it, and hear it just the same. Not physically, of course, but spiritually.

When I was about 22 years old, I dated a young lady from Ethiopia. She was a good-natured person. She was kind to everyone and had a very pleasant disposition. As a Christian, the first thing I wanted to know before I asked her out on a date was if she was Christian. I worked the third shift at Walmart in the electronics department, and she worked the second shift at the front registers as a cashier. She was a fairly attractive young lady, but I was not interested in her or anyone else at the time. It was an older lady, a deeply devout Christian from El Salvador who thought her, the girl at the front of the store, and I, the guy at the back of the store, would be a match.

After weeks of telling her I was not interested, she pleaded with me to swallow my pride and ask the young lady out on a date. After much thought, I finally agreed. But I only had one question for my older sister in the Lord. "Is she a Christian?" "Absolutely," she said. "I would never recommend you date someone that wasn't." "OK." I responded. "I'll ask her out." So, I did ask her out, and we got to know each other a little over the next few weeks. On about our fifth or sixth date, we went to a restaurant and sat at a booth by the window. I don't remember anything about the restaurant or the food, but I will never forget that conversation!

Somehow, I started talking about how I came to the Lord. It was not unusual for me to talk about God. In fact, I talked about Him a lot. And since we both were Christian, and I was a preacher, we talked about Him quite often. But something was different this time. It felt different. I not only shared my testimony. I also shared how thankful I was to not have to spend eternity separated from God. I lamented to her about how the countless number of our peers who cross our paths every day don't know the joy that we've tasted, having our sins forgiven and our unrighteousness cleansed by the blood of Jesus.

I went on a five-minute or so rant about the seriousness of our generation hearing the real gospel. And how they would hear it if more of us started preaching it to them so they could get saved. After getting off my soap box, I felt like a burden was lifted, and I could finally stop talking and start eating my food. There was no doubt in my mind that she, too, shared my sentiments and would also give me her point of view on the subject at hand. I was not prepared for what was about to unfold. I ate my food in silence for the next few minutes and thought nothing of how unusually quiet she was. Until I noticed that she was no longer eating her food. I was about to ask her why she wasn't eating, only to see her eyes welling up with tears.

She looked as if she had just heard the news of a loved one passing away. "What's wrong?" I said. Completely oblivious to what had just taken place and that I was the one responsible for it. Like a famished hostage would reluctantly but desperately request a drink of water from their captor, she said, "Tell me that again, please." "Tell you what?" I said. Still clueless as to exactly what she was referring to. "Tell me how you became a Christian?" I had just finished telling her how I had become a Christian, and would gladly have done it again. But I felt that was not really the question she was asking.

So, I asked her a question instead. "How did you become a Christian?" Without hesitation, she said, "I've always been a Christian." My entire family is Christian, so I was born a Christian. I was startled by my realization. But grateful, for her sake, that the mercy and grace of God had led me to this discovery. For I not only realized she wasn't a Christian. At that moment, I realized that she didn't know she wasn't a Christian. "How am I going to break this news to her?" I thought. I ran through a couple of scenarios in my head, all of which ended badly. Then, I finally mustered up the courage to ask her, "Do you know what it means to be saved?" "No." She said. "I've heard you say it before, but I figured it's just another word for Christian."

I explained to her that the name Jesus is the English translation of the Hebrew word Yahshua. It means that God has become our salvation. "You mean to save the sinners?" She said. "Yes," I replied. "Do you know who the sinners are?" Of course," she said. "All of the bad people." "Absolutely! The sinners are all the bad people. And the bad people are you and I and everyone else in the entire world." I replied. Even if I had hit her with a sledge-hammer, it probably wouldn't have been as shocking as that statement was to her. "Everyone!" She retorted. "How? No, no, no!!! That can't be! Everyone is going to hell! What about the good people who don't murder, steal, and break laws? Everyone is born in sin." So I explained, "The Bible says that all have sinned and come short of the glory of God. The Bible says that there is none righteous, not even one person."

I explained to her something I've been preaching since I was a teenager. It's a phrase I coined that simplifies the subject of sin. "A sinner is not a sinner because he sins; rather, he sins because he's a sinner." I explained to her the revelation I received about what David said in Psalms 51: *"I was born in sin, and in iniquity my mother conceived me."*

After murdering Uriah the Hittite and sleeping with his wife Bathsheba, David is finally realizing that, "I am NOT a murderer because I murdered, and I am NOT an adulterer because I committed adultery. I committed murder because I'm a murderer, and I committed adultery because I am an adulterer. I am not what I am because of what I did, but I did what I did because I never allowed God to deal with the issue of what I am."

I explained to her, "You are not who you are because of what you do, but you do what you do because of who you are. And when God, by the power of His Holy Spirit, changes who you are; it will empower you to change what you do." She pleaded with me to stop talking and give her the solution for her sinful condition "What do I do? Can God save me?"

Once she realized she was a sinner, she immediately recognized her need for a savior. I told her that God became a man in the person of Jesus Christ and died for her sins. I told her that if she would repent and believe in His death, burial, and resurrection, that He would save her and bring her into His Kingdom. I prayed with her, and as she cried, I watched a transformation take place. I saw her come out of the kingdom of darkness and into the Kingdom of God. She said she felt completely different. While I was talking, she said she felt as if her sin was so heavy it was going to crush her. After we prayed, she felt completely light and free. The burden of sin and guilt was lifted from her shoulders.

The Kingdom of God is spiritual, so the only way to enter into it is spiritually. Not intellectually or emotionally, but spiritually. There's not a magic prayer that gets you into the Kingdom. There's a glorious person. His name is Jesus! When you repent from you and everything you know, and trust in Him, and everything He knows, His kingdom will invade your life. Then He will immerse you in His Spirit, and the Kingdom of Heaven will live in your heart. You will be alive in God, and your spiritual senses will be activated.

You'll still make mistakes, but the more you continue to submit to Him, the more you will exchange your way of thinking for His way of thinking. Then more and more, His Kingdom will come, and His will, will be done on Earth as it is in Heaven. That's how you experience the King, and the power of His Kingdom. You'll be a true ALIEN, not of this world! Living on Earth, but born from Heaven, sent into the world to bring people into the Kingdom you now belong to!

HOPE IS NOT

WISHFUL THINKING.

CHAPTER 4
SEEING THE KINGDOM

Everyone who is born of Heaven has inherited the ability to see the Kingdom of God, just as we who are born on Earth have the ability to see Earth. Not from a distance, but up close and personal. On a daily basis, we interact and interface with it. Because of our physical bodies' compatibility with Earth, we rely on it for our food and sustenance.

Even so, on a daily basis, we are able to interact and interface with the heavenly Kingdom we have been born into. Because of our human spirit's compatibility with the spirit world, we rely on it for our spiritual food and continual sustenance.

In chapter two, we learned that if we get a revelation of what's going on where God is, it will change what's going on where we are. In chapter three, we learned that only those who are born of Heaven can see the Kingdom of Heaven. When we merge those thoughts together, what it teaches us is that the man who is from Heaven can see Heaven, and the man who can see Heaven can change Earth. In the *Marvel* comic story of Thor, the god of thunder, Thor is frequently transported back and forth from Asgard, a type of Heaven, to Midgard, a type of Earth. His father, Odin, the god of all the nine realms, sends his son moving throughout his kingdom to establish order and keep peace. The movies *Thor* and *Thor: The Dark World* depict in vivid detail this fictional god of thunder's commute from Asgard to wherever his father chooses to send him.

Needless to say, my wife and I went to the movies to see both of these films. Or should I say, I went, and she came with me. This is most often the case with action-packed motion pictures. Sitting in that dark theater, stuffing my face with heavily-buttered popcorn and delectable mouthwatering Goobers, I couldn't help but to notice the spiritual similarity between this movie and the Kingdom of God. Just as Odin, the god and king of everything in this fictional story sends his son to establish order and bring peace, so the God of the Bible, the King of all Kings sends His Son into the world to establish His order and bring His peace.

That's why Jesus said in Matthew 5:9, *"Blessed are the peacemakers, for they will be called the children of God."* One of the major characteristics of a child of God is their ability to bring divine order in the midst of confusion. It is God's order that dispels confusion and brings His peace.

What impressed me the most about the movie was how every time Thor was on a mission in one of the nine realms, he maintained a connection with Asgard. There was never a moment when he was not in communication with the realm from which he was sent. On one occasion, upon completing an assignment, he said, "Heimdall, whenever you're ready." Communicating to Heimdall, the all-seeing and all-hearing guardian sentry of Asgard who stands on the rainbow bridge, that he is ready to be transported back to Asgard. Wherever he was, he could always sense the presence of Asgard, his father's home. It seemed as if that was even more real to him than wherever he was physically.

He didn't just know about the kingdom that sent him; he could see it whenever he wanted to. All he had to do was "say the word," and he would immediately be transported there. There are many Christians who know they belong to the Kingdom of God, but they can't see it. They don't know that all they have to do is ask, and God will grant it to them.

You Have to See

Proverbs 29:18 KJV

Where there is no vision, the people perish.

Sometimes, it's just as important to know what something is not as to know what it is. Learning what it's not gets you just that much closer to understanding what it is. Such is the case with the biblical concept of vision.

Vision has often been taught as a plan for one's future. Or as a set of goals a person has determined to accomplish. That is not the biblical definition of vision.

Planning and goal setting is the inevitable result of having vision. But it's not vision itself. Vision simply means to see. When someone has vision, it means they can see. If they have good vision, it means they see really well. So, when the Bible says, "Where there is no vision, the people perish," it can also be translated as "Where the leaders can't see, the people have no guidance."

The NIV says, *"Where there is no revelation, people cast off restraint..."*

The NLT says, *"When people do not accept divine guidance they run wild..."*

The ESV says, *"Where there is no prophetic vision the people cast off restraint..."*

Vision is insight into the spirit world concerning God's intentions for the physical world. That is what real vision is. When leaders can't see in the realm of the Spirit concerning God's intentions for the realm of the Earth, the people they're leading have no divine direction for their lives. I know you might say, "But Rohan, they have the Bible." Let me show you why the Bible alone is not enough.

As a loving and attentive parent, you may have a well-thought-out plan for all of your children's lives. But if you can't see into the spirit world concerning God's intentions for them, then you have no real vision. And if you have no real vision, then it's highly likely that your children have no real guidance concerning the direction. God wants them to go in life. If Joseph and Mary only raised Jesus, according to the written Word of God, but had no spiritual insight that He was the Messiah, they would've had no vision for who He really was; therefore, they would've lacked the ability to provide true guidance for Him. As a matter of fact, if that was the case, they would have spent most of His life misunderstanding Him. In order for them to raise him effectively, God had to provide both of them with spiritual insight concerning who He really was. Mary knew the Divine identity of the child she was pregnant with because of a visitation from an angel. Joseph knew he was supposed to marry Mary, even though she wasn't pregnant with his child because the angel assured him the child was the son of God. Joseph also knew what to do to protect his family because he was warned in a dream to move his family to Egypt because his son's life was in danger.

If Zechariah, the priest, had not had an angelic visitation that informed him that he was going to have a son and that his son would be a prophet, then it is quite likely, according to tradition, that he would have raised his son to be a priest as he was. It was his revelation of what his son was supposed to be that gave him the ability to raise him to become that.

Luke 1:59-63 NIV

[59] On the eighth day they came to circumcise the child, and they were going to name him after his father Zechariah, [60] but his mother spoke up and said, "No! He is to be called John." [61] They said to her, "There is no one among your relatives who has that name." [62] Then they made signs to his father, to find out what he would like to name the child. [63] He asked for a writing tablet, and to everyone's astonishment he wrote, "His name is John."

Zechariah and Elizabeth were able to fight for the prophetic identity of their son because they had a revelation of who their son was supposed to be before he was born. If Zechariah had never received that revelation, he and his wife would have never had the ability to silence the voices that were about to unintentionally misidentify their son. The same was the case with Rebekah, Isaac's wife.

Genesis 25:22-23 NLT

But the two children struggled with each other in her womb. So she went to ask the Lord about it. "Why is this happening to me?" she asked. [23] And the Lord told her, "The sons in your womb will become two nations. From the very beginning, the two nations will be rivals. One nation will be stronger than the other; and your older son will serve your younger son."

Because Rebekah went to God in prayer about the struggle that was happening in her pregnancy, she found out from the Lord, three extremely important things about her pregnancy.

The first thing she found out was that she was pregnant with twins.

The second thing she found out was that two manner of nations were going to be born from these twins.

The third thing she discovered was that her oldest son would serve her youngest son. In other words, her son, who would be Jacob was destined for something great.

Had she not received that revelation, it's quite likely that she wouldn't have fought so hard for Jacob to fulfill his destiny.

It's not enough just to raise our children according to the written Word of God; we must also allow the Holy Spirit to reveal to us His specific intentions for them as well. And it doesn't mean that He will give you the same level of detail He gave to these parents in the scriptural examples I just gave. But it does mean that we as parents need to seek God for spiritual insight into the identity and destiny of our children.

In every aspect of your life, your plans and your goals must be based on your vision. But if you can't see what God has planned for you, then what exactly are you planning for yourself? This is why we need vision. In order to live for the King, we have to see what's happening in His Kingdom!

What Does *Seeing* Look Like?

When I say you have to see the spirit world, I'm not suggesting that you have to literally have open visions of God on His throne, surrounded by angelic activity. I'm rather suggesting that seeing is the overwhelming awareness of what the Heavenly Father wants and how the Holy Spirit is moving concerning you. That's so good! Let me say it again. Seeing is the overwhelming awareness of what the Heavenly Father wants and how the Holy Spirit is moving concerning you.

John 5:19 NLT

"So Jesus explained, "I tell you the truth, the Son can do nothing by Himself. He does only what He sees the Father doing. Whatever the Father does, the Son also does."

I often say it's easy to be what you see. If I never knew my father, I would still grow up to look like him, but I would not necessarily grow up to be like him. It was knowing him my entire life that caused me to be able to effortlessly emulate many of his traits. Because it's easy to be what you see. God does not just want His children to look like Him; He wants us to be like Him. When we use religious language such as "Praise the Lord," "Have a blessed day," "God is good, all the time, and all the time God is good," to the world around us, we look like God. We don't necessarily appear godly. We just appear to be attempting to associate ourselves with God.

But when we pray, study the word, obey it, do to others as we'd have them do to us, and develop godly relationships, we begin to get a vision of the things that are happening in God's Kingdom. That's when it becomes easier for us not just to look like God but to be like God. We won't just say, "Have a blessed day." We'll also bless someone by praying for God to help them in their area of need or help them meet that need. We won't just say, "God is good," we'll demonstrate His goodness through our random acts of kindness. It's not enough to belong to God. You also have to behold God.

Simply being related to my parents was not enough to guarantee that I would grow up with their values and ideals. I had to observe them and then imitate (put into practice) what I observed. As His children, we must observe our Heavenly Father! We must see Him in His word, in our worship, and in our relationships with one another. Then we must imitate, emulate, and put into practice all that we observe. The more we seek Him, the more we'll see Him, and the more we see Him, the easier it will be to be like Him.

No Vision No Faith, No Faith No Vision

In the KJV, Hebrews, Chapter 11, Verse 1 says, *"Now faith is the substance of things hoped for, and the evidence of things not seen."*

What most of us call faith today is really just wishful thinking disguised in faith's clothes. I can't tell you the amount of times people have said things to me along this line, "Pastor, I'm scared to death about this move that I'm getting ready to make. I really hope it works out. I guess I'm just going to have to step out by faith." What they're really saying is, "I have no clue what I'm doing, so I'm going to give it my best guess, take a flying leap into the Unknown, and pray that God catches me!" The truth is, if you've lived long enough, you, too, have felt like this at some point. I know I have felt this way several times in my life. But I also know that this is not what faith is.

Faith is not trying your best to believe God in spite of not hearing His voice and feeling His presence. It's believing God because you've heard His voice and felt His presence in spite of the fact that your circumstances don't concur with your spiritual revelation. Faith is to your spirit what your eyes are to your body. It's your ability to see where you're going and what God has for you.

2 Corinthians 5:7 NOG

"Indeed, our lives are guided by faith, not by sight."

Our lives are not guided by what we can physically see but by what we can spiritually see. When we see things spiritually, we understand everything in our world from that spiritual perspective. Faith is spiritual vision. When you have no vision, you have no faith.

There is no such thing as "blind faith." Faith, by definition, sees. If your faith does not see, then it's not faith. It's wishful thinking, or a positive attitude about the future. But real faith is real vision into the purposes and plans of God. It doesn't mean that you see everything, or understand everything you see. It just means that you saw what you needed to see to respond in obedience to what God wants you to do.

Hebrews 11:1 NLT

"Faith is the confidence that what we hope for will actually happen; it gives us assurance about things we cannot see."

Faith is confidence based on the spiritual evidence for something you cannot yet physically see. When lawyers cross-examine witnesses, they are taught to speak to them with confidence, even if they don't have a sure way to discredit their testimony. When police officers are interrogating suspects, they are trained to seem certain of the fact that the suspect committed the crime. But how much more confident would that police detective or cross-examining lawyer be if they actually had evidence that proved the case they were trying to argue? They wouldn't have to try to behave confidently; they would inevitably be confident.

Especially if they were getting ready to present that evidence in the next few minutes. No one would be able to convince them of anything that was contrary to the evidence they had in their possession. This is the way that faith works. When something is revealed to you about God, or God reveals something to you about something He plans to do, that revelation is spiritual evidence. When you hear it, or you see it, regardless of the circumstance of life that seems contrary to what God has revealed to you, your revelation is the spiritual evidence that fuels your confidence. That's why Romans 10:17 says (and I paraphrase for context and clarification) that faith comes by hearing the word of God or hearing a word from God. A word from God gives you spiritual insight into His world. Without this, you have no vision. And if you have no vision, you have no faith.

The Framework of Faith

Notice that Paul calls faith the substance of things hoped for. The NLT translation says it's the *"confidence that the things we hope for will actually happen."* The word hope does not mean the same thing it means to us in our modern-day vernacular. I often say that poor vocabulary makes for bad theology and such is the case here. When most of us use the phrase, "I hope...," what we mean is, "I've got my fingers crossed that things are going to turn out okay." That's far from the biblical concept of hope. The Bible refers to the return of the Lord Jesus back to this planet as "the blessed hope." Titus 2:13

That doesn't mean that we've got our fingers crossed in hopes that Jesus might really come back for His Church one day. It means that we have an *assurance* that Jesus will come back for His Church. Hope is the foundation of faith. It's the bone structure and framework of faith. Hope is not wishful thinking. It's a reasonable expectation based on spiritual evidence that the things you're believing God for is going to come to pass.

Faith is not when I hope that God will do a certain thing. That's wishful thinking dressed up in faith's clothes. Faith is when I have hope that God will do a certain thing. Faith is not when I know that God can do what He said He will do. Faith is when I know that God will do what he said he will do because He revealed it to me.

The Godkind of Faith

Mark 11:22-23 NLT

Then Jesus said to the disciples, "Have faith in God. [23] I tell you the truth, you can say to this mountain, 'May you be lifted up and thrown into the sea,' and it will happen. But you must really believe it will happen and have no doubt in your heart.

This is not what the original manuscript says. It actually says, "Have the faith of God…" or "Have the God kind of Faith…" That changes the connotation of the scripture. Because it begs the question, "What is the God kind of faith?"

It's the kind of faith that sees as God sees and then says what it sees in order to bring it to pass. This explains why the text says, "…whoever will say to this mountain, be removed and cast into the sea, will have whatsoever he says."

God sees all things, so, therefore, everything He says is because of what He's previously seen. It doesn't mean that God Himself needs to have faith. It rather means that real faith (the faith God intended for us to have) gives us the ability to see as He sees and the authorization to speak on His behalf. Because you have no authorization to speak on His behalf if you cannot see as He sees.

Real faith (the faith God intended for us to have) gives us the ability to see as God sees and the authorization to speak on His behalf. This principle is very simple yet extremely profound! If you see what God sees, and feel what He feels, then you will say what He says, and see it come to pass.

Seeing the Throne Room

As I said in the second chapter, I believe God wants us to be where He is.

But I think His greatest desire is for His people to create an environment that is so similar to where He is that it makes it possible for Him to be where we are. That's why the prayer the Lord taught His disciples to pray in Matthew 6:5-15 and Luke 11:1-13 starts by talking about where God is and then ends up talking about where we are. The point is that the person who can see heaven is qualified to change Earth. We see this truth in the prayer the Lord taught His disciples to pray.

Matthew 6:9-15 NIV

"This, then, is how you should pray:

"'Our Father in Heaven,

hallowed be Your name,

[10] Your Kingdom come,

Your will be done,

on Earth as it is in Heaven.

[11] Give us today our daily bread.

[12] And forgive us our debts,

as we also have forgiven our debtors.

[13] And lead us not into temptation,

but deliver us from the evil one.'

[14] For if You forgive other people when they sin against You, Your heavenly Father will also forgive you.

[15] But if You do not forgive others their sins, Your Father will not forgive Your sins.

The prayer starts out with the majesty and holiness of God in Heaven and ends up with how we are to treat one another here on Earth. Because once we behold His world, it will change our world. Whenever I'm teaching on prayer, the first thing I like to say is prayer does not begin with what you say; it begins with what you see. Most believers say a lot of things in prayer, but they don't see a lot of things when they pray. I'd rather see a lot of things about God in prayer and say nothing than to say a lot of things to God in prayer and see nothing.

The manner in which the Lord taught us to pray demonstrates that principle. Let's look at the first part of the prayer. The prayer starts out:

Our Father in Heaven- We first have to see who God is and where He is. The first step to changing your world is beholding Him in His. The first thing you have to know is that because you have been born into His Kingdom, God is your Father. Even if you didn't have a good relationship with your father, the concept of fatherhood is something we all as humans can relate to.

Who lives in Heaven- Who God is as our Father is something we can relate to. It gives us the right to approach Him with confidence. Just as a child has the right to approach a parent and expect the parent to shower them with love and affection, so we have the right to approach our heavenly Father, expecting forgiveness, mercy, grace, and love.

But immediately after telling us that He is a person we can relate to, He informs us that He lives in a place we can't relate to. Heaven. Once again, another example of the genius of God! We can relate to the person but can't readily or mentally relate to the place. So, in order to understand more about the person, we can immediately relate to (God), we must investigate a place we can't readily relate to (Heaven).

This brings clarification to Isaiah 2:3, which says in the NLT,

"Come, let us go up to the mountain of the Lord, to the house of Jacob's God. There, he will teach us His ways, and we will walk in His paths."

It's the determination to make a departure from the things of this world, and elevate into the environment of His Majesty that teaches us His ways and enables us to walk in His paths. The prayer continues:

Hollowed be Your name—It can be translated as holy is Your name. Or may we keep Your name holy. Holy means different than, other than, and separate than. May we realize that though we are related to you, you are someone and something we will never be able to relate to.

When I was a little boy, I was only interested in who my father was as it related to me. The older I became, the more I developed an interest in who He was as an individual. Not in His ability to be anything to me or do anything for me. But I just became more interested in who He was as a person. My interest in who my father was, as it related to me, was vital to my childhood development. But had it not grown beyond that, I would not be able to have a healthy relationship with him today. All of our conversations would consist of me talking about me. And if I eventually got around to talking about him, it would only be in light of what he has done for me or something he could do for me.

Many of us, as believers, are only interested in who God is as it relates to us. We're not interested at all in who He is as it relates to Him. For example, He told Moses in Exodus 3:6, NLT, *"I am the God of your father—the God of Abraham, the God of Isaac, and the God of Jacob."* Then, in Exodus 3:14, He told him *"...I am who I am. Say this to the people of Israel: I am has sent me to you."*

In other words:

GOD: "I not only want you to know who I am as it relates to you. I also want you to know that I am something you will never be able to relate to. I told you that I am the Lord God of your fathers because I want you to know that you are related to me. But I also told you, "I am that I am" because I want you to know that I'm holy, and though you are related to me, you will never be able to relate to who I really am."

My father's name is Arlington Peart. As most children do, I always called him "Daddy," and I always saw him as such. Because that's who he is as it relates to me. Daddy is not who he is; it's who he is to me. There's a difference. He's never had a problem with me calling him Daddy, because that's how I relate to him, but he thinks of himself as Arlington.

God understands when we call Him God, or Father, or Savior, or Healer, because He knows that's how we relate to Him. Though we call Him God, God is not what He calls himself. He calls Himself Holy! That's why the angels in closest proximity to Him can't call Him anything else but Holy. Because the word holy is the Hebrew word, Kadosh. It means exclusive to, separate from, other than, and different than. In the Bible, the idea of holiness corresponds with one-ness. That's why the prophet Isaiah refers to God as "The Holy One of Israel" 25 times. So, in its purest definition, holy can be translated as ONLY!

So, when the incredible beings around God's throne are calling Him Holy, they're not saying clean and pure. They're saying only, only, only!!! "You're the ONLY ONE like You." This is what Isaiah saw in the throne room of God, recorded in Chapter Six of his prophetic masterpiece. He saw the holiness, otherness, and awesomeness of God! God in indescribable magnificence, and terrifying majesty! Surrounding God's throne are six magnificent angelic creatures called Seraphim. They each have six wings and use four of them to cover their faces and feet. They use the other two to keep flying around the throne. And with loud voices, they shout the same phrase back and forth to one another. Kadosh Kadosh Kadosh Adonai Tz'vaot M'lo Khol Ha'aretz K'vodo. "Holy, Holy, Holy, the Lord of Hosts, the whole Earth is filled with His Glory."

In essence, they are exclaiming-

"In all of space and every dimension of time, you are the only one like you!!" That's why we call God's Spirit the Holy Spirit. Because He's the "Only Spirit," from which life proceeds and healing wisdom, knowledge, and understanding are generated!! Angels are holy because God made them holy. In his original state, man is holy because God made us holy. We are made only for His purpose and pleasure. But God is the only one that is holy, holy, holy! The reason is that there are many angels and many men. But there is only one God!! For though He can make us like Him; He can never make another Him!! WOW!! Hallelujah!! Holy are you, Lord. Sorry, I just had to take a quick praise break.

As one great theologian, Dr. R.C. Sproul, puts it, "God is not just holy to the imperative degree, He is holy to the superlative degree." The imperative degree is the second degree. The statement is imperative when something is said twice in a row in the Bible. "Truly, truly I say to you …" whatever follows is imperative truth. That means it's something we should pay very close attention to. However, when something is said in Scripture three times in a row, it is superlative truth. It is truth of the highest and most supreme importance. God is not just holy; He is holy,

holy, holy! He is holy to the highest degree! I call the holiness of God the *'onliness'* of God. He is the *only* One like Him.

When the Seraphim go around the throne, and they see God's wisdom, you would think they would stop shouting holy, and start shouting wise, wise, wise is the Lord God almighty! When they see His grace; you would think they would stop shouting holy and start shouting gracious, gracious, gracious is the Lord God almighty.

When they see that He is love, you would think they would stop shouting holy and start shouting love, love, love is the Lord God Almighty. But the reason they keep shouting holy when they see how lovely He is, is because they're overwhelmed by the fact that He is the only one from which this immeasurable amount of love proceeds. He's the only one from which this unfathomable, incalculable grace, wisdom, and love flows.

The reason they see His Power, and they don't shout powerful, powerful, powerful, is because they're declaring, "You're the only one as powerful as You are." Not only is He the only being to possess all of these attributes, but He's the only being that is the source of all of His attributes. Whew! This is why, just like Isaiah, we must see God high and lifted up in Heavenly majesty. Even if we are not transported to the Throne room, as Isaiah was, we must have a vision of the throne room in our hearts.

Notice that toward the end of Isaiah Chapter Six, the Lord asks who will go on His behalf, and then Isaiah, the one who is beholding God on His throne, says, "Here I am, send me." It's no coincidence that the one who saw God was sent to represent Him.

Isaiah had a vision. That vision wasn't a set of goals he intended to accomplish. It was insight into the Spirit realm. He then developed his goals to reach his generation based on that vision. He could only be sent as a representative of the Kingdom after seeing the King's majesty.

A Boring God

This is why I doubt very seriously that many professing Christians in our generation have had a real encounter with God. I don't say that in a judgmental sense but rather as a point of observation. Too many Christians today are either casual about God, indifferent toward God, or just plain bored by the thought of God. A.W. Tozer said, "Any man or woman on this Earth who is bored and turned off by worship is not ready for Heaven." I take it a step further. If worship bores you, you're not worshipping. One day, I was telling a guy about God when he told me, "I could never do the God thing; it's just too boring." I asked him. "How boring is it, knowing everything, being everywhere, traveling through time, and having unlimited power to use whenever and however you choose, and to use that power to create things that have never existed before? God's not boring, sir; our lack of interest in a being like that makes us boring!" He was stunned by my response. He said, "I never thought about it like that before." I thought to myself, "I bet you didn't."

From time to time, God's children may present Him in a boring way. But that is not God's fault, and He should never be blamed for it. It's the fault of His representatives. And we should be blamed for doing a poor job of adequately representing God. It's impossible to see God and be bored. The world lacks an interest in God because they've never seen Him. If the truth be told, the church lacks an interest in God because we've never seen Him. That's why we make our lives more about us than we do about Him. It's because our pursuits reflect our interests. We are more interested in us than we are in Him because we have seen more of us than we have seen of Him. The goals we set are about us because our vision is of us. Our goals are based on our vision. The reason many Christians today don't have a vibrant and healthy relationship with God is because they're far more interested in themselves than they are in Him.

Throughout the years, I've been acquaintances with good-natured and easygoing people. Some of these people I've been very fond of. But the reason many of those relationships never progressed toward significant friendships was not because I unearthed some troubling news about them. You see, though, I'm a preacher and can do my fair share of talking; I'm actually a very good listener. I love to listen to what people have to say.

But when you listen to people who claim to be your friends, talk about themselves for hours on end and never once stop to ask you how you're doing, the conclusion that you come to is that they are far more interested in themselves than they are in you. This makes it difficult to ever have a true friendship with someone like this.

You can remain casual acquaintances, but that's about as far as it can go. The cross of Jesus is proof that God loves us more than we could ever imagine. But no matter how much you love someone, it's difficult to have a relationship with someone who is not really interested in you. I believe that this is why God's relationship with the children of Israel was so strained throughout history.

Because though they were his children, for the most part, they were only interested in who He was as it related to their health, wealth, and safety. They were religious, pious, and serious about their many customs and rituals. But if truth be told, they were not really interested in God. That's why Moses had a much better relationship with God than they did. It was because he was not only interested in what God could do for him, he was actually interested in who God was.

By and large, the Church today is not much different than the Children of Israel. We are God's children. But we are really only interested in who God is as it relates to our health, wealth, and safety. In as much as it pains me to say this. Most of us who claim to follow Jesus are not really interested in Him.

This is easy to see when we examine our Sunday morning worship services. They look a whole lot like the worshipers and very little like the One being worshipped. Out of the thousands of Churches in America, how many of those pulpits are filled with pastors teaching their congregations to seek God until they have a life-altering encounter with the Holy Spirit? How many of those sermons being preached and songs being sung are filled with the things that God is interested in? Or are most of them filled with well-meaning, good-hearted pastors and worship leaders curtailing their messages and music to the interests of their congregants?

The proof that you are interested in God is that you share His interests. And His interests, therefore, become your pursuit. God is interested in filling the whole Earth with His glory by seeking and saving

THAT which was lost. That's why the anthem of the Seraphim around the throne is twofold.

1. Holy, Holy, Holy is the Lord God Almighty. - *That's who God is.*

2. The whole Earth is filled with His glory - *That's what God wants.*

They are constantly declaring to one another their revelation of who God is and what He wants. Think about that for a moment. The beings that are in closest proximity to God's presence are constantly declaring their revelation of who He is and what He wants! Wow! Their mouths are constantly filled with their revelation of His identity and His interests! That thought makes me want to throw up my hands and give God the glory He alone deserves! I think we should pause once again right here for a meditation and praise break. Hallelujah!! How great is our God!!

This is how it ought to be with us in the Kingdom of God. I believe that the reason God gave Isaiah such an encounter was not only to propel his prophetic ministry to a brand-new level, but to reveal a pattern of how God establishes His glory and government in the midst of His people!

The citizens of the Kingdom who will remain in closest proximity to the presence of the King are the ones who have devoted their lives to do what the six-winged Seraphim are doing in Isaiah Chapter Six. That is continually exchanging with one another, the revelation of who God is and what He wants.

Isaiah 6:3

They were calling out to each other, "Holy, holy, holy is the Lord of Heaven's Armies! The whole earth is filled with his glory!"

Notice that they are not telling God seated upon His throne that He is holy. They are speaking back and forth to one another about the holiness, otherness, oneliness, and awesomeness of the One seated upon the throne. This is a picture of how God establishes His throne, kingdom, dominion, and government in the midst of those who sing his praises to one another.

Ephesians 5:19 NKJV

"Speak to one another in psalms and hymns and spiritual songs, singing and making melody in your heart to the Lord..."

The reason the mouths of the Seraphim are constantly declaring the identity and interests of the one seated upon the throne is because the hearts of the Seraphim constantly desire to be more consumed with His identity and interests. They're not declaring what they hope to desire. Their desire is the reason they're declaring these things.

I often say it this way. Their declaration is because of their revelation. Their praise is not the consequence of some obligatory religious duty. It's the inevitable result of a revelatory response. They are SEEING magnificent things in His presence, so they can't help but SAY what they SEE!

The reason that most people are not interested in God is because they've never seen Him. They've never been in His presence and had an encounter with Him that truly rocked their world and shook them to their core. The Seraphim are excessively and radically worshiping God! But they are not doing it out of some religious obligation to His instructions. They're doing it because of their helpless addiction to His presence! In other words, they can't help it! This kind of worship is not best described as the Seraphim's religious duties. It should rather be described as the only appropriate response of any being with this level of proximity to the Presence of God! If you and I were this close to the one seated upon the throne, we couldn't do anything but worship him either.

When anyone or anything gets this close to God, it's impossible not to drown in the rushing rivers of His righteousness and become consumed by the raging fire of His holiness! Daniel fell as dead before an angel. John the beloved also fell as dead before an Angel. Isaiah became unglued in the throne room and said, "Woe is me, for I'm undone." There is no such thing as remaining indifferent while being burned by fire, hit by a tsunami, struck by lightning, or frantically trying to evacuate a building that is being toppled by an earthquake.

Everyone, regardless of personality, preference, cultural upbringing, ethnicity, or socioeconomic background, will significantly react to any of these events. By the same token, there is no such thing as remaining indifferent while being burned by the fire of God's holiness, hit by the tsunami of His love, and struck by the lighting of His truth! Excessively outrageous worship is the only appropriate response to the overwhelming revelation of His identity! And if you can't give God that, then you have not seen Him! And if you have not seen Him, no wonder you are bored with whatever it is you see; you were created to behold His beauty. Seeing Jesus and being bored, indifferent, or casual about Him is impossible. And it is impossible to truly represent Him until you've seen Him.

ROHAN PEART

ALIENS ARE GOD'S STRATEGY FOR EVANGELISM!

CHAPTER 5
THE FIRST INVASION

As a pastor and Bible teacher, one of my greatest passions is to break the Word of God down in such a way that it makes seemingly complex theology easy to understand.

That's why when I wanted to teach people about the Kingdom of God, I sought the simplest way to do it without compromising the integrity of the message. Hence, the acronym for the word aliens.

Awakened

Lives

Invading

Every

Nation

Supernaturally

I created this acronym to become an outline of how God intended His Kingdom to come to the Earth. This acronym illustrates that in a way that I believe is easy to understand. Until Jesus comes back, the only way God's Kingdom comes to the Earth is through awakened and anointed lives worldwide, invading their sphere of influence with the supernatural power of God.

ALIENS are God's strategy for evangelism! That's why Jesus said go into the world and make disciples of all nations. The Kingdom only comes when we who are a part of it go into the world to bring the Good News of the Kingdom of God to everyone.

God's Blueprint for Evangelism

The idea for this alien invasion is demonstrated in the incarnation of God in the flesh (Jesus Christ), but it did not start with the incarnation. The idea is also evident in the prayer that Jesus taught His disciples, but it didn't start there either.

It started back at the beginning, in the book of Genesis, with the creation of man. That was the first alien invasion. If we want to understand what the intention of God is in redemption, we must first seek to understand what the intention of God was in creation. If we want to understand what the intention of God is in the last Adam (Jesus Christ), we must first seek to understand what the intention of God was in the first Adam (in the Garden of Eden).

Ecclesiastes 1:9 says this: *"The thing which has been is that that shall be. And that which was done is that which shall be done."* In other words, if you want to know how it's going to be in the end, you have to investigate how it was in the beginning. Because whatever God is trying to do in the second Adam, Jesus Christ is what He was trying to do in the first Adam, in the garden.

Until we discover what He was trying to do, we will never understand what He is trying to do now. Before we can understand the aliens God wants us to be, we must first understand the alien He created Adam to be. So, let's take a look at the first alien invasion. Genesis 1:26-28.

It tells us that God created man in His own image and after His own likeness. It says that God gave him dominion over all the works of his hands. The birds of the air, the beasts of the field, and the fish of the sea were all under man's authority.

Man's responsibilities were to be fruitful and increase in number, fill the Earth, and govern it. He was given authority over everything above him, everything around him, and everything underneath him. He was sent to the Earth for the purpose of bringing everything above Him, around Him, and underneath Him under the government of Heaven.

This was God's plan for how to bring the Kingdom of Heaven into the Earth. It was to put the Kingdom in a man, then put the man in the Earth.

A.L.I.E.N.S.

Brilliant! Absolutely brilliant! This is the genius of God. But it gets even better than this. After God put the Kingdom in the man, then put the man in the Earth, He commanded the man to reproduce himself. The mere act of reproducing himself would automatically extend the boundaries of God's kingdom. Because the man already bore the image of the King, therefore his offspring would also reflect the King's image.

This is still God's plan for how to bring His Kingdom into the Earth. It's God's blueprint for evangelism. To put the Kingdom in a man, put that man in a community, then instruct him to reproduce himself by bringing others into the Kingdom. It amazes me how hard we work to bring people into the Kingdom of God. Churches go on entire soul-winning campaigns. I remember when I was younger, I went to a church that didn't bring one soul to God all year long. But at the end of every year, they would pay a lot of money to bring in special guest speakers to preach "hell" so hot you could feel its breath nipping at your heels.

Right before the altar call, the guest speaker would make every believer scour the congregation to find anyone who did not know Jesus as Lord and Savior, and even offer to walk them down to the altar. We almost had to interrogate people to find out if they were not Christians.

Nothing about this felt organic to me. It all felt forced and contrived. Not to mention awkward and embarrassing. After the evangelist was unsuccessful at getting anyone to respond to the invitation; he would lay a heavy guilt trip on all the nonbelievers. He would say things like, "What if you leave here tonight and get in a car accident and die on your way home? You would go straight to hell because you never came down and made it right with God." I used to have a visceral physical reaction when I heard preachers say things like that. I would cringe because It was so painful. It was like watching a train wreck and praying that there were no casualties. It's amazing to me that it still hasn't dawned on those who preach that way that there is not one recorded sermon in the book of Acts where the apostles, or anyone else, preached about hell as a way to introduce sinners to the Kingdom of heaven. But all through the book of Acts, we see them preaching about King Jesus and His glorious Kingdom. The fear of hell has never kept anyone from going there. Only the love of God has delivered people out of the flames of hell.

After such meetings, I would go back to my school on Monday, and minister to more of my classmates than I ever saw come to God in those revival meetings. I'm not knocking conferences, convocations, crusades, and special services. I believe in having them. Any reason to gather together and lift up the name of Jesus is a good one. But I do believe we have made evangelism painful and difficult when God intended for it to be joyous and effortless. How joyous and effortless, you ask?

As joyous and effortless as two people in love being intimate with one another and getting pregnant. Adam never had to struggle to reproduce the image of God on Earth. In fact, this was the easiest part of his assignment. He didn't need a *"Reproducing the Image of God"* class. All he had to do was what came naturally. You don't have to be a rocket scientist to figure out what I'm alluding to. He just had to be intimate with his wife. That's all.

The relationship between Adam and Eve is a picture of the relationship between Christ and the Church. Adam represents Christ. The woman represents the Church. Just like Adam, all the woman had to do was what came naturally. What is that?

1. Be intimate with her husband

2. Give birth to the image of God that came from the act of intimacy

This was the divine strategy for alien invasion. Intimacy and reproduction. Because reproduction is the inevitable result of intimacy. This divine strategy is God's blueprint for evangelism. When the Church, through prayer, Bible study, and worship, gets intimate with her heavenly Husband, she will effortlessly reproduce the image of God.

Now, let's push the pause button right here for a minute to make something very clear. I am in no way suggesting that we, as believers and followers of Jesus Christ, are supposed to have some sort of mystical, metaphorical, sexual relationship with God. That's just flat-out weird, blasphemous, and, as a Bible College Instructor of mine used to say, "goofy."

I am, however, referencing the Word of God when it parallels and compares the relationship between Christ and the church to a relationship between a husband and a wife. Just as the natural union between a husband and a wife creates natural offspring, the spiritual union between Christ and the church creates spiritual offspring. As long as we keep this in its proper context and don't go too far with the language or imagery, there is nothing weird or strange about drawing that parallel.

One day, years ago, before my wife and I had children, I was on the phone with a dear man of God and spiritual father who pastors a great church in Georgia. As we were wrapping up our conversation, I asked him if he would keep my wife and me in prayer because we were trying to have children. To which he replied, "You do know how that happens, don't you?" Caught off guard and not really understanding the question, I stuttered a little in my response. "Uhm, ahh, how what happens?" "How babies happen," he said. There was an awkward pause for about four seconds, and then we laughed hysterically. He was joking, of course, but the truth is often said in jest. If a couple wants to have children, but they are not frequently, and consistently, intimate with one another, then all the praying in the world will not increase their chances.

We don't need soul-winning seminars to win souls. No more than we need baby-making seminars to reproduce children. All we need to do is spend time with the one who sent us into the world until He transforms us into His image. We need to spend time worshipping Him and reading His word until our affections burn with a passion for the things, He's passionate about. Then, we will truly become spiritual because we will be totally submitted to the process of becoming like Him! It's that simple.

Then, when we encounter those who don't know God, instead of trying so hard to convince them to "turn or burn," we will joyfully and effortlessly transfer to them what He has transferred to us. Because transformed lives transform lives. That's how the first alien invasion took place, and that's how it's been taking place ever since. By God's people getting intimate with God and giving birth to His image.

Image and Likeness

God created Adam in His image and in His likeness. God's image is His nature and attributes. God's likeness is the outcome of having His image or maturing the image of God within you. In other words, because man was created with God's nature and attributes, He is very much like God. He is designed to think and function like God thinks and functions.

Adam couldn't help the measure to which he bore God's image. That was God's investment. Adam had nothing to do with that. Adam, however, had everything to do with the degree to which he nurtured the divine nature and attributes within him. God's image was revealed in Adam's design. God's likeness was revealed in Adams development.

He had nothing to do with the way he was designed but everything to do with how the attributes of God within him developed on a daily basis. This is called the likeness of God and is the most important aspiration of human life.

To be like Him!

Romans 8:29 NLT

For God knew His people in advance, and He chose them to become like His Son so that His Son would be the firstborn among many brothers and sisters.

God's goal in becoming a man, as we'll discover a little later, wasn't just to save him from sin. It was ultimately to restore him back to functioning for the purpose for which He created him. That's the reason God became like us. It was to give us the ability to become like him. He didn't just live, die, and resurrect for humanity. He lived, died, and resurrected as humanity to give mankind the ability to become what He is.

I like to say it this way: The God of men became the Son of man so that the sons of men could become the sons of God. He became the body of Christ and died so that we could become a part of his body and share in His divine life. It's when we nurture the divine nature within us that we become more and more like Jesus. Because once again, God's image was revealed in Adam's design, but God's likeness was revealed in Adam's development.

This is what I mean when I talk about spiritual intimacy. It's not about having some spooky romantic rendezvous with Jesus. That's goofy. It's about spending time in the presence of God and immersing yourself in the word of God until your mind is filled with the thoughts of God and your heart is overflowing with the love of God. After a while, without even trying, you're becoming more and more like Jesus. Every day, without even trying my five-year-old son RJ is becoming more and more like me. He can't help the fact that he has my nature. That was given to him at the time of his conception. But every day he spends with me, that nature is nurtured, and he grows in my likeness and in my ways. In the same way, the believer cannot help but have the nature of God within them. But the more time they spend with God in prayer and studying His word; that nature is nurtured. And without even trying, they become more and more like Him.

What is God like?

2 Corinthians 3:16-18 MSG

Whenever, though, they turn to face God as Moses did, God removes the veil, and there they are—face-to-face! They suddenly recognize that God is a living, personal presence, not a piece of chiseled stone. And when God is personally present, a living Spirit, that old, constricting legislation is recognized as obsolete. We're free of it! All of us! Nothing between us and God, our faces shining with the brightness of his face. And so, we are transfigured much like the Messiah, our lives gradually becoming brighter and more beautiful as God enters our lives and we become like him.

God does not enter our lives so that we can feel goose pimples and sing amazing grace. There's nothing wrong with singing that song or feeling those goose pimples. But that's just not the reason. God enters our lives.

He enters our lives so that we can become like Him. This begs the question, how do we know if we're becoming like Jesus? On one occasion, when Jesus warned against false prophets, He taught his disciples an easy way to recognize them.

Matthew 7:16-20 NLT

You can identify them by their fruit, that is, by the way they act. Can you pick grapes from thornbushes or figs from thistles? [17]A good tree produces good fruit, and a bad tree produces bad fruit. [18]A good tree can't produce *bad fruit, and a bad tree can't produce good fruit. *[19]* So every tree that does not produce good fruit is chopped down and thrown into the fire. *[20]* Yes, just as you can identify a tree by its fruit, so you can identify people by their actions.*

You can judge whether you are or are not becoming more like Jesus, based on the fruit your life bears. As Jesus said, you can identify people by their actions. You are not like Christ if your life does not exhibit Christ-like behavior. If I'm becoming more like Christ, there is bad fruit I shouldn't be bearing. The Bible lists them here:

Galatians 5:19-21 NLT

*When you follow the desires of your sinful nature, the results are very clear: sexual immorality, impurity, lustful pleasures, *[20]*idolatry, sorcery, hostility, quarreling, jealousy, outbursts of anger, selfish ambition, dissension, division, *[21]*envy, drunkenness, wild parties, and other sins like these. Let me tell you again, as I have before, that anyone living that sort of life will not inherit the Kingdom of God.*

If I'm becoming more like Christ, there is good fruit I should bear.

Galatians 5:22-23 NLT

[22]But the Holy Spirit produces this kind of fruit in our lives: love, joy, peace, patience, kindness, goodness, faithfulness, [23]gentleness, and self-control...

These traits and characteristics are the fruit that should be growing from the tree of my life when I'm becoming more like Jesus. Notice that the scripture doesn't say "fruits," plural, but it rather says "fruit" singular. The Holy Spirit is not producing multiple fruits from the tree of your life. He is, rather, producing one singular fruit. So why does the Scripture list multiple characteristics of the Holy Spirit, if it's only a singular fruit. If you read it again, you might notice that there really is only one fruit listed. That fruit is Love. So why, then, are their eight other traits of the Holy Spirit listed if love is the only one? I believe it's because love is the primary fruit of God's Spirit and everything else flows out of God's love.

A.L.I.E.N.S.

1 John 4:8 TLB

But if a person isn't loving and kind, it shows that he doesn't know God— for God is love.

God is love. And everything He does is fueled by His love. All of His actions are fueled by His love. Even His very wrath is the consequence of the degree to which He loves. If, at the very least, the majority of the thoughts, words, and actions of a child of God are not fueled by the love of God, then that child of God is not godly. Because the epitome of godliness is Love! Not man's love for God because man can't love God until the love of God dwells in his heart. But the epitome of godliness is God's love in man extended to all men. It's the love of God. That's godliness.

Romans 5:5 NLT

...we know how dearly God loves us because He has given us the Holy Spirit to fill our hearts with His love.

One of the essential reasons for the giving of the Holy Spirit is listed here. To fill our hearts with God's love. Only the Holy Spirit in us can give us the ability to love like God does. It's His love in us, loving people through us.

Jesus said in John 13:35, NLT *"Your love for one another will prove to the world that you are my disciples."*

The thing that proves to the world that you are a follower of Jesus Christ is when the Love of God consumes your thoughts, words, and actions. You can't grow in His likeness if you aren't growing in His love. It's not your ability to love God that proves to the world that you're a lover of God. It's your willingness to allow God to love your brothers and sisters in Christ through you that proves to the world that you're a lover of God. But you can only allow God to love through you after you have allowed God's love to dwell in you. And God's love only dwells in those who have accepted the perfect way that God loves us, it's His perfect love that casts out all fear.

1 John 4:18 TLB

We need have no fear of someone who loves us perfectly; His perfect love for us eliminates all dread of what he might do to us. If we are afraid, it is for fear of what he might do to us, and shows that we are not fully convinced that he really loves us.

One of my favorite Christian thinkers, who happens to also be a scientist, Dr. Caroline Leaf, wrote a book that I highly recommend. It's entitled *Who Switched Off My Brain?* She said, "The brain is wired for love." The brain is designed to be consumed by the love of God. It is healthy when it is and unhealthy when it's not. When the all-consuming love of God captures your imagination, the fire of His holy love burns away all negativity and transforms you into the likeness of that love.

Even the entire law of God is fulfilled in the love of God. When God created man He didn't give him a Bible; He gave him His word, His presence, and a wife. The reason that's what He gave him is because He wasn't starting a religion; He was beginning a relationship. The reason for the Bible is that man no longer had a relationship with God, so he needed a roadmap back to God's presence. God didn't create man and give him a list of rules; He created man and gave him a life filled with relationship and revelation. And the reason most people would rather live by a list of rules is because they are overcompensating for their lack of relationship and revelation.

The message of the Bible is not to make us legalistic for God; it's to make us lovers of God. Legalism was introduced to human society the moment that God's love no longer dominated the human heart.

Galatians 5:14 NIV

For the entire law is fulfilled in keeping this one command: "Love your neighbor as yourself."

Notice, again, the same principle: Everything else that God tells us to do flows out of love. So, if you don't have love, then nothing else matters. Because you can't have any of God's other attributes without it. Because God is love.

A.L.I.E.N.S.

Matthew 22:34-40 NLT

But when the Pharisees heard that he had silenced the Sadducees, with his reply, they met together to question him again. [35] One of them, an expert in religious law, tried to trap him with this question: [36] "Teacher, which is the most important commandment in the law of Moses?" [37] Jesus replied," 'You must love the Lord your God with all your heart, all your soul, and all your mind.' [38] This is the first and greatest commandment. [39] A second is equally important: 'Love your neighbor as yourself.' [40] The entire law and all the demands of the prophets are based on these two commandments."

These are the very words of our Lord and Savior Himself. At that time, the law and prophets were the whole Bible. The New Testament didn't exist yet. So, what Jesus was actually saying was that the entire word of God is based on God's love. Not rules and religious duties. It's based on God's love for us, in us, and through us. That's amazing!

Romans 13:8-10 TLB

Pay all your debts except the debt of love for others—never finish paying that! For if you love them, you will be obeying all of God's laws, fulfilling all his requirements. [9] If you love your neighbor as much as you love yourself, you will not want to harm or cheat him, or kill him or steal from him. And you won't sin with his wife or want what is his, or do anything else the Ten Commandments say is wrong. All ten are wrapped up in this one: to love your neighbor as you love yourself. [10] Love does no wrong to anyone. That's why it fully satisfies all of God's requirements. It is the only law you need.

When the love of God consumes our thoughts and burns in our hearts, it will give us the desire for spiritual intimacy so that we can effortlessly give birth to God's image on Earth. This was the reason for the first ALIEN. The first life that God awakened and anointed to invade the Earth was supposed to reproduce God's image and mature in His likeness day by day. Tragically, this mission was compromised in its infancy, and a second invasion had to take place. The first ALIEN was disobedient to his Creator and, therefore, failed to accomplish what he was sent to do.

The second ALIEN would have to finish the task. The fate of the human race depended upon it. The second ALIEN would be Heaven's last attempt at accomplishing the impossible. It was a mission too crucial to send a celestial ambassador, heavenly emissary, or a mere mortal. This time, the Lord of Heaven would have to do it Himself. Because of love, He would have to become them. Because of Love, He would have to redeem them. Because of Love He would transform them into His likeness, by first being transformed into theirs. A mortal He would have to become.

CHAPTER 6
THE SECOND INVASION

Redeeming the Purpose

God became a Man to redeem His people. For the angel said to Joseph, "You will give him the name Jesus, because he will save his people from their sins." Mathew 1:21. God loves people. But that was not the only reason He became a man. The reason so many believers are ineffective after they become believers is because they think the only reason God saved them was so that they could be saved.

God became a man to redeem his people. But He also became a man to redeem his purpose. Jesus told Zacchaeus, "The Son of man came to seek and to save that which was lost." Not just those who are lost, but THAT which was lost. He redeemed us to restore us back to the purpose He created us to accomplish.

The first invasion was unsuccessfully attempted by the first Adam. The second invasion was successfully completed by the second Adam, AKA the last Adam. He is the last because, after Him, there would be no need for another. God's goal in becoming a man wasn't just to save us from sin. It was ultimately to restore us back to functioning for the purpose for which He created us. That's the reason God became like us. It was to give us the ability to become like him.

Mission Impossible

Adam did not just fail to obey God. His failure to obey God prevented him from being able to mature in the likeness of God. And the less like God he was, the more incapable he was of bringing the Earth under the government of Heaven. So he was excommunicated from God's presence, and disqualified from operating in his ambassadorial role.

Since God is not only creative in nature but also redemptive in nature, He did not destroy the first Adam but rather came up with a plan to redeem him. This plan is what I call the second invasion. It was the incarnation of God in the flesh. In the first invasion, God put His Kingdom in a man and put that man in the Earth in order to establish His Kingdom in the Earth realm. That man's disobedience to God disconnected him from God, thus rendering him incapable of establishing the Kingdom he was no longer a part of. The second invasion was similar to the first, because the objective was the same. Bring all things under the government of Heaven!

But two things would be different. This time, there would be an added mission. Before all things could be brought under the government of Heaven, the power of darkness that seduced God's highest form of creation into rebelling against their Creator would have to be broken.

The second thing that would be different was that the one executing the mission would be God Himself. For an ordinary man, this mission would be impossible. But the Creator and Alien King had already accomplished this impossible mission before the foundations of the world were established. He would now have to manifest His masterpiece. Like a loving father whose only son had been kidnapped and held hostage for ransom, God took this to heart. This was personal. And He would handle it personally.

God As Us, Us As God

The God of men became the Son of Man and died on Earth, so that the sons of men could become the sons of God, and live in Heaven. God became like us so that we could become like Him. He came to where we are so that we could go to where He is. He descended to Earth as a man to give God the legal right to live in the Earth. He ascended to Heaven as a man to give man the legal right to live in Heaven. He died as if He were us, so that we could live as if we were Him.

The entire point of the incarnation is that God became like us so that we could become like Him. I call it the "The-anthropological revolution." It's a complex-sounding theological term, but it's much simpler than it sounds. "The" means God. "Anthrop" means man. It is God coming to Earth to be with man so that man could go to Heaven and be with God. It's a complete revolution. But I love to simplify seemingly complex theological truths. It can be summed up like this. You didn't know how to be you, so God had to become you in order to be for you, the "YOU" that He originally created you to be. How great is that? It's that simple.

Jesus Christ is the Divine human. The only flesh that has been anointed and authorized by the Holy Spirit with the legal right to stand in the very presence of God! He's the perfect man! Romans 3:10 says, *"No one is righteous, not even one."* The idea here is that there is no one living that has the capacity for righteousness.

1 John 2:1 NLT

My dear children, I am writing this to you so you will not sin. But if anyone does sin, there is One who will go between him and the Father. He is Jesus Christ, the One who is right with God.

Jesus Christ is the perfect man. The only flesh that has been anointed and authorized by the Holy Spirit with the legal right to stand in the very presence of God! He is the only human living with the capacity for righteousness. Therefore, He is the only one qualified to make us right with God. He is the only human accepted in Heaven because the only flesh that God accepts is His own! God will never accept any other human than the one He became to make every other human acceptable in His sight. That's why He ascended up to Heaven in human form so that everyone who becomes a part of His flesh is automatically authorized to be where He is.

Hebrews 1:3 TLB

God's Son shines out with God's glory and all that God's Son is and does marks him as God. He regulates the universe by the mighty power of his command. He is the one who died to cleanse us and clear our record of all sin and then sat down in the highest honor beside the great God of Heaven.

Colossians 3:3-4 NLT

...you died to this life, and your real life is hidden with Christ in God. ⁴And when Christ, who is your life, is revealed to the whole world, you will share in all his glory.

The only lawful claim that one has for being in God is that they are with Christ. And Christ is their life. Christ is the one who escorts you into the Presence of the Father. Being with Him gives you the authority and ability to safely navigate the corridors of God's presence. He is the grace and truth that allows you to explore the aspects of God's nature that would kill you if He wasn't with you!

Invasion for Access

Five steps constitute this The-Anthropological Revolution.

1. He came to Earth as us, to be for us what we couldn't be for Him. (John 1:14)

2. He shed His blood for us to provide us with the Divine DNA that would make us a new creation. The body of Christ. (Ephesians 2:13)

3. He went back to Heaven as us, to give us the legal right to live in His heavenly Presence. (Romans 8:34-35)

4. He sent His Holy Spirit to us to give Himself the legal authority to live on the Earth. (John 16:7)

5. So now, God is us, acting on our behalf in Heaven, and we are Him, acting on His behalf in the Earth. We are not actually Him, but we are given the legal right by him to stand in His stead. (1 John 4:17)

Men had no access to God. And because of sin, God had no access to men. Isaiah 59:1-2. So, God had to become a man so that as fully God and fully man, He would be qualified to bring men into the presence of God and bring God into the presence of men. The first Adam's sin caused mankind to lose access to the Creator's Presence. The second Adam's sacrifice caused mankind to regain access to the Creator's Presence. The incarnation was all about access! It was God becoming the gateway for Heaven to have access to the Earth and the inhabitants of earth to have access to heaven.

The Perfect Man

Religion is man's idea of the perfect God. Which is idolatry because it's man making God in his image. The Incarnation is God's idea of the perfect man, because it's God showing man what man was always supposed to be. Religion is God in man's image, but Jesus Christ is Man in God's image. The only way that any man can truly be accepted by God is when he accepts God's version of the perfect man! The man, Christ Jesus.

So here are your options: accept God's version of the perfect man so that God can start living his life through you. Or try your best to live a life without God that equals God's standard of perfection. It's impossible, yet it's what every religion has tried to do since the beginning of time. However, the reason that Jesus is the only one who can please God is because Jesus is God, and God is the only one capable of meeting His own demands. Why are we trying to do for God what He already did for us? We would feel foolish in our human efforts to please God if we knew what the Bible really has to say about the finished work of Christ.

Hebrews 10:1-14 NLT

The old system under the law of Moses was only a shadow, a dim preview of the good things to come, not the good things themselves. The sacrifices under that system were repeated again and again, year after year, but they were never able to provide perfect cleansing for those who came to worship. ²If they could have provided perfect cleansing, the sacrifices would have stopped, for the worshipers would have been purified once and for all time and their feelings of guilt would have disappeared. But instead, those sacrifices actually reminded them of their sins year after year. ⁴ For it is not possible for the blood of bulls and goats to take away sins. ⁵That is why, when Christ came into the world, he said to God, "You did not want animal sacrifices or sin offerings. But you have given me a body to offer. ⁶You were not pleased with burnt offerings or other offerings for sin. ⁷Then I said, "Look, I have come to do your will, O God— as is written about me in the Scriptures.'" ⁸First, Christ said, "You did not want animal sacrifices or sin offerings or burnt offerings or other offerings for sin, nor were you pleased with them" (though they are required by the law of Moses). ⁹Then he said, "Look, I have come to do your will." He cancels the first covenant in order to put the second into effect. ¹⁰For God's will was for us to be made holy by the sacrifice of the body of Jesus Christ, once and for all time. ¹¹Under the old covenant, the priest stands and ministers before the altar day after day, offering the same sacrifices again and again, which can never take away sins. ¹² But our High Priest offered himself to God as a single sacrifice for sins, good for all time. Then he sat down in the place of honor at God's right hand. ¹³ There, he waits until his enemies are humbled and made a footstool under his feet. ¹⁴ For by that one offering he forever made perfect those who are being made holy.

Notice that the Scripture says that we are being made holy, but we are already made perfect (complete) by the offering of His body. You don't have to try to please God. You just have to allow the only human that God is pleased with to live His life through you.

Galatians 2:20 NLT

I have been put up on the cross to die with Christ. I no longer live. Christ lives in me. The life I now live in this body, I live by putting my trust in the Son of God. He was the One Who loved me and gave Himself for me.

The Two Adams

1 John 5:12 NIV

Whoever has the Son has life; whoever does not have the Son of God does not have life.

If you don't have the Son of God, you don't have life because the Son of God is the only human alive! There is only one life to live. That is the life that God wants to live through you. Man originally had eternal life when God first created him, but because of disobedience, he lost his life.

Romans 5:12, 15-19 NLT

This is what happened: Sin came into the world by one man, Adam. Sin brought death with it. Death spread to all men because all have sinned . . . death had power over men from the time of Adam until the time of Moses. Even the power of death was over those who had not sinned in the same way Adam sinned. Adam was like the One who was to come. [15]God's free gift is not like the sin of Adam. Many people died because of the sin of this one man, Adam. But the loving-favor of God came . . . by one Man Jesus Christ, God's Son...through Adam came sin and guilt. But the free gift makes men right with God. Through One, Christ, men's sins are forgiven. [17]The power of death was over all men because of the sin of one man, Adam. But many people will receive God's loving-favor, the gift of being made right with God, and have power in life by Jesus Christ. [18] Through Adam's sin, death and hell came to all men. But another Man, Christ, by His right act makes men free and gives them life. [19]Adam did not obey God, and many people became sinners through him. Christ obeyed God and made many people right with Himself.

The first Adam died and brought death into the world. The last Adam died, conquered death by resurrecting from it, and brought life into the world. So, every human being is either dead in the first Adam, or alive in the last Adam. There is no in-between. You either have the Son of God, which is the life of God in human form. Or you are dead in the first Adam and have no life at all.

The entire human race was in the first Adam when he sinned, so we all sinned with him. When he sinned, he inherited death, so we all died with him. The segment of the human race that believes in Christ was in Christ when He died and was resurrected. So, when He died, he killed the aspect of us that keeps us from living. When He resurrected, we who died with Him emerged from the tomb as a brand new species of being. We emerged as ALIENS, alive by the divine power and nature of our Alien King!

1 Corinthians 15:20-23 NLT

But in fact, Christ has been raised from the dead. He is the first of a great harvest of all who have died. [21]So you see, just as death came into the world through a man, now the resurrection from the dead has begun through another man. [22] Just as everyone dies because we all belong to Adam, everyone who belongs to Christ will be given new life. ²³ But there is an order to this resurrection: Christ was raised as the first of the harvest; then all who belong to Christ will be raised when he comes back.

Jesus didn't die to kill Himself; He died to kill the aspect of you that keeps you from living. He didn't just resurrect so He could Live; He resurrected to bring your true identity back to life.

Alive for Dominion

Jesus was resurrected, not just so we can live, but so that we can live the way God originally intended us to live. With complete authority!

Genesis 1:27-28 NLT

So God created human beings in his own image. In the image of God He created them; male and female He created them.²⁸ Then God blessed them and said, "Be fruitful and multiply. Fill the Earth and govern it. Reign over the fish in the sea, the birds in the sky, and all the animals that scurry along the ground."

Psalm 8:3-8 AMP

When I view and consider Your heavens, the work of Your fingers, the moon, and the stars, which You have ordained and established,⁴ What is man that You are mindful of him, and the son of [earthborn] man that You care for him? ⁵ Yet You have made him but a little lower than God, and You have crowned him with glory and honor. ⁶You made him to have dominion over the works of Your hands; You have put all things under his feet:⁷ All sheep and oxen, yes, and the beasts of the field, ⁸ The birds of the air, and the fish of the sea, and whatever passes along the paths of the seas.

Dominion is Divine authority to rule over your domain. That is what God gave man when He created him. He authorized him to govern the Earth and everything in it.

Psalm 115:16 NLT
The heavens belong to the Lord, but he has given the earth to all humanity.

Heaven is God's house, and earth is man's house. God is the Lord of heaven, but He has made man the Lord of the earth. Heaven is perfect and glorious because God, who rules heaven, is perfect and glorious. Earth is imperfect and decaying because man, who rules earth, is imperfect and decaying. The condition of heaven is a reflection of the One who is in authority over it: God. Heaven is filled with righteousness, peace, and joy. The condition of the Earth is a reflection of the one who is in authority over it: Man. Earth is filled with violence, immorality, and confusion.

There is nothing in Heaven that God has not authorized to be there. Because He is the ultimate authority in that environment. There is nothing on Earth that Man has not authorized to be here. Because we are the ultimate authority in this environment. And whatever we tolerate, we give permission to:

"Reign over the fish in the sea, the birds in the sky, and all the animals that scurry along the ground."

God gave Adam authority in three realms.

1. The Sea - Everything underneath Him
2. The Sky - Everything above Him
3. The Ground - Everything around Him

Adam lost this authority when he sinned against God.

Genesis 3:17 NLT

And to the man He said, "Since you listened to your wife and ate from the tree whose fruit I commanded you not to eat, the ground is cursed because of you. All your life, you will struggle to scratch a living from it.

Notice that God did not curse the ground. He simply informed the man that the ground was now cursed because of his disobedience. The ground became cursed because man was made from the ground, and the material of the earth responded to the fallen nature of the one who was in authority over it. The environment became dysfunctional when the identity of the man responsible for governing it was contaminated.

A dysfunctional environment does not always create a dysfunctional man. However, a dysfunctional man will always create a dysfunctional environment. The best thing that can happen to a dysfunctional environment is that it comes under the authority of a functional man. Because truly functional men transform chaotic environments.

Since Adam had authority over everything underneath him, above him, and around him, he also had authority over the serpent. So, as soon as Adam saw that the serpent that was under his authority was being used by another authority to oppose God's authority, he should have immediately expelled the spirit that was functioning in a manner that he did not authorize. Our responsibility on the Earth is to maintain order. And to use the word of God to call things that are out of order back into order.

When man fell, he lost the authority he once had over his environment. So, Jesus came not only to redeem us but to restore our authority back to us again.

Matthew 28:18 TLB

He told his disciples, "I have been given all authority in heaven and earth."

God created man and gave him authority over the Earth. Man sinned and lost that authority. So God became a man to restore man's authority over the earth back to him again. God could not take back man's authority for him unless he did it as him. So Jesus' authority over the Earth is as us and for us. Our authority over the Earth is in Him and with Him. The only legal way for God to regain man's authority on the Earth is as man and for man. The only legal way that man can regain his authority is in Christ and with Christ.

2 Corinthians 5:17 NKJV

Therefore, if anyone is in Christ, he is a new creation; old things have passed away; behold, all things have become new.

Romans 8:17 NLT

And since we are his children, we are his heirs. In fact, together with Christ, we are heirs of God's glory.

Those of us who are in Christ are also with Christ. Because we are in Christ, we have inherited His identity. Because we are with Christ, we have inherited His authority. In Him, we have His nature, and with Him, we bear His name. Because we are in Him, we know our identity. Because we are with Him, we walk in authority.

Jesus did not take back authority to keep it for Himself. He took it back to share it with us.

Luke 12:32 NLT

"...don't be afraid, little flock. For it gives your Father great happiness to give you the Kingdom.

Luke 10:19 NLT

Look, I have given you authority over all the power of the enemy, and you can walk among snakes and scorpions and crush them. Nothing will injure you.

Adam didn't need a course in demonology; he just needed to understand his dominion. If he understood it, he would have responded to the devil in the earth the same way that God responded to Lucifer in heaven. He would have kicked him out. We don't need a course in demonology; we just need to understand our identity in Christ and our authority with Christ.

Two Adams and a Fig Tree

Mark 11:12-14, 20-25 NLT

The next morning as they were leaving Bethany, Jesus was hungry. [13] He noticed a fig tree in full leaf a little way off, so he went over to see if he could find any figs. But there were only leaves because it was too early in the season for fruit. [14] Then Jesus said to the tree, "May no one ever eat your fruit again!" And the disciples heard him say it...

[20] The next morning as they passed by the fig tree he had cursed, the disciples noticed it had withered from the roots up. [21] Peter remembered what Jesus had said to the tree on the previous day and exclaimed, "Look, Rabbi! The fig tree you cursed has withered and died!"

²² Then Jesus said to the disciples, "Have faith in God. ²³ I tell you the truth, you can say to this mountain, 'May you be lifted up and thrown into the sea,' and it will happen. But you must really believe it will happen and have no doubt in your heart. ²⁴ I tell you, you can pray for anything, and if you believe that you've received it, it will be yours. ²⁵ But when you are praying, first forgive anyone you are holding a grudge against, so that your Father in heaven will forgive your sins, too."

Genesis 3:6-7 NLV

The woman saw that the tree was good for food, and pleasing to the eyes, and could fill the desire of making one wise. So she took of its fruit and ate. She also gave some to her husband, and he ate. ⁷ Then the eyes of both of them were opened, and they knew they were without clothes. So they sewed fig leaves together and made themselves clothing.

The first Adam ate from a tree that stripped him of God's glory and disinherited his eternal life. Then, he used another tree to cover his shame. The second Adam cursed the fig tree that the first Adam used to cover his shame. Then, He died on a tree to restore God's glory and re-inherit eternal life. What Jesus was doing in cursing the fig tree, is actually symbolically reversing the curse. Adam covered himself with fig leaves because he was naked of the glory of God that previously clothed him. Ever since then, man has been using materialistic means to compensate for his lack of spiritual covering.

Jesus cursing the fig tree was a prophetic announcement to the earth realm that the time had come for man to be restored to his former glory. Therefore, he will no longer need his environment to compensate for his lack of glory. God never intended for you to be covered in the things around you; He intended for you to be the covering for the things around you.

This announcement is one that we, as sons of God, must also reinforce. We must also curse the fig tree. That means to use the word of God in our mouth to announce to creation: "Man will no longer seek his environment for covering. For man has once again become the covering for his environment."

The Bible says that the next day, the disciples saw that the fig tree had withered and died. And they all looked at the fig tree in great amazement. Even Peter was so astonished by it he pointed it out to Jesus as if it were something exceptional. Then Jesus said to all of them, "Have faith in God." In the original manuscript, it actually reads, have the faith of God. "...you can say to this mountain, 'May you be lifted up and thrown into the sea,' and it will happen."

What Jesus was saying was this, "You think that what I have done to this fig tree is exceptional. But you don't realize that if you tell even this huge mountain to get up and cast itself into the sea, and you really believe, the mountain will have to obey you."

You have been given the responsibility to take authority over everything in your environment. All the way from a seemingly insignificant fig tree to a magnificent, molded mountain. Your words have the ability to move things in your environment out of place or move things in your environment into place. So "Have the faith of God." When you see as God sees, and you say what God says everything in your environment will respond to you the same way it responds to Him.

Genesis 2:19 NLV

Out of the ground the Lord God made every animal of the field and every bird of the sky. He brought them to the man to find out what he would call them. And whatever the man called a living thing, that was its name.

As much as God likes to do certain things for us, He is far more enthralled with watching us do things like Him. He created all things with His word, and He loves to watch us use our words to impact the world around us. Just like we are fascinated as parents to watch our children, behave like us, God is fascinated as our heavenly Father to watch His children behave like Him.

Psalm 119:89 NKJV

Forever, O Lord, Your word is settled in heaven.

The word of the Lord is settled in heaven, because God settled it there. But the word of the Lord only becomes settled in the Earth when we use our authority in Christ to restore God's order to our world. That's why the scripture says, "Death and life are in the power of the tongue..." Proverbs 18:21. It doesn't just mean that death is negative, and life is positive. It also means that we have the ability to speak death to things that shouldn't be living and speak life to things that shouldn't be dead.

When Jesus cursed the fig tree, He put things back in their right order. He was God as man, reasserting man's authority over creation. He did this by speaking death to the cycle of co-dependency that started at the fig tree. After he reversed the curse, he taught them that if you see as God sees and say what God says, then everything in your environment will respond to you the same way it responds to God. They saw how the fig tree responded to the words of Jesus, and they were amazed. Jesus then says to them, have God's faith. "Because if you have God's faith, you will see as God sees, and then you will say as God says. And the way this fig tree responded to me is the same way this mountain will respond to you."

The Blood of Heaven

Leviticus 17:11 NLT

...for the life of the body is in its blood. I have given you the blood on the altar to purify you, making you right with the Lord. It is the blood, given in exchange for a life, that makes purification possible.

Hebrews 9:11-12 NLT

So Christ has now become the High Priest over all the good things that have come. He has entered that greater, more perfect Tabernacle in heaven, which was not made by human hands and is not part of this created world. [12]With his own blood—not the blood of goats and calves—he entered the Most Holy Place once for all time and secured our redemption forever.

Galatians 4:4-7 ESV

But when the fullness of time had come, God sent forth his Son, born of woman, born under the law, [5]to redeem those who were under the law, so that we might receive adoption as sons. [6]And because you are sons, God has sent the Spirit of his Son into our hearts, crying, "Abba! Father!" [7]So you are no longer a slave, but a son, and if a son, then an heir through God.

If this were a novel, it would be similar to the short story book I wrote called *The Tale of the Alien King*. I urge you to buy that book if you haven't already. That's a shameless plug, by the way. The story would read like this:

The body of the Alien King, Yeshua, from the planet Shamayim (shaw-mah'-yim) was formed by the Holy Spirit in the virgin womb of a Hebrew girl in Nazareth. He smuggled His heavenly nature into the sinful planet of Earth in the Divine DNA contained within His blood cells. The cells within His physical blood literally contained the spiritual nature of God. So, when the blood of Yeshua was shed; it not only washed away our sins, but it also created a brand-new species of Being. The life of Heaven in physical form. The most valuable substance in the entire universe is the blood of King Yeshua because it is the very life of the Heavenly Father in physical form. Before his blood was shed, He was the only one who had access to the life of God within him. After his blood was shed, the whole world gained access to that life. It was like top secret classified government intel being leaked (pun intended) to the whole world on how to become a real-life *Marvel* comic superhero. The soil of the Earth from which mankind was molded violently convulsed with shockwaves of nostalgic ecstasy from tasting the blood of its own Maker. The blood was spilled, earth drank it, the veil was torn, and access was granted. Invasion accomplished.

IT OUGHT TO BE JUST AS NORMAL FOR YOU TO BE IN THE PRESENCE OF ANGELS, AS IT IS FOR YOU TO SIT AT THE KITCHEN TABLE WITH YOUR WIFE AND CHILDREN.

CHAPTER 7

THE BEST OF BOTH WORLDS

How one aspect of God's creation is seamlessly woven into another is quite poetic. The Moon, for example, is related to the Sun. It needs the light of the Sun to shine against the blackness of the night sky. It also needs the blackness of the night sky to reveal the brilliant light of the Sun that's always shining upon it. Even bodies of water are related to one another and, at times, flow in and out of each other. Silent streams and rushing rivers that flow from high hills and majestic mountains often merge together with other streams of water to run down into lovely lakes, salty seas, and raging oceans. These things are not by accident; they are by order. By God's order, to be exact. He designed it that way.

When we observe how something was created, we understand why it was created. When we understand its design, we understand its destiny. The fish of the sea are designed with fins because they are destined to swim. The beasts of the field have legs because they are destined to walk upon the land. The birds of the air have wings because they are destined to fly. Their design reveals their destiny.

The same is true for man. The fabric of mankind's destiny and design are seamlessly interlaced. Man's overall destiny is to manifest the Kingdom of Heaven within him into the Earth. Therefore, God designed him to do just that. When we learn how we, as humans, were created, we will understand why we were created, and recognize how easy it is to accomplish what we were created for.

Heaven's Breath, Earth's Dust

When I was a little boy in Baltimore, MD, there was a commercial for Ziploc bags that used to come on television. I'm sure there have been many Ziploc bag commercials since their invention, but this one was memorable to me. As I recall, it was of a little boy holding an opened Ziploc bag. One side of the opened mouth of the bag was yellow. The other side was blue. The boy placed some contents in the bag, and started to seal it shut. As he was doing that, the blue and yellow colors merged together to make a green seal. He then said, "Yellow and blue make green." I thought that was a cool commercial. Not only was it advertising a new product, it was giving the consumer an education in the science of merging colors. Two colors came together to make one color. Blue never ceased to be blue, and yellow never ceased to be yellow. They both came together to make a color that neither of them was before they merged as one. After seeing that commercial I never forgot that yellow and blue make green. We see this same principle in Genesis chapter two and verse seven. Just as yellow and blue make green, thousands of years ago, God's breath, and Earth's dirt made the greatest, literally "groundbreaking," invention of all time. Neither substance ceased to be what it was, but each one, seamlessly woven into the other, came together to make something brand new.

Genesis 2:7 NKJV

And the Lord God formed man of the dust of the ground, and breathed into his nostrils the breath of life; and man became a living being.

God, who is the master scientist, took two materials. His breath and the earth's dust, and He used those resources to make mankind. The breath of God is the material of Heaven, and the dust of the ground is the material of Earth. God took the material of Heaven, and the material of Earth, then merged them both together to create man. So that means that man is the material of Heaven and the material of Earth perfectly, harmoniously co-existing together in the same environment! Wow! Read that statement a couple more times, then take a praise break. What an awesome God we serve! No wonder David said in Psalm 139:13-14, NLT, *You made all the delicate, inner parts of my body and knit me together in my mother's womb. Thank you for making me so wonderfully complex!*

Your workmanship is marvelous—how well I know it.

Man is the wonderfully complex, marvelous workmanship of God! Do you realize what you are? Not who you are, but what you are? We'll deal with knowing who you are in chapter 9, entitled, "The Real You." But do you realize what you are? Do you realize the way you were designed to function? If you knew what you were, you wouldn't settle for what you've been! If you knew that you were Heaven and Earth, designed to inhale the Presence of God in prayer, and exhale the power of God in your everyday life; you wouldn't settle for the scraps of a mediocre existence. This is why David said in Psalm 8:4, and I paraphrase, "What is man that you are both mindful of him, and even go as far as to visit him."

In other words, "What is it about man that causes the God of the universe to constantly have him on His mind and care enough about him to stop by and visit him all the time?" There has got to be something about man that causes God to make this big of a deal about him.

That something is that man is God's son. He is Heaven and Earth, perfectly harmoniously co-existing together in the same place. God makes such a fuss about us, because He knows what we are. If we knew about us what He knows about us, we wouldn't live our lives like it was no big deal. And we certainly wouldn't settle for less than His plan and purpose for us.

When I illustrate this point in a sermon, I often walk to one side of the platform and say, "Heaven was all the way over here, where it was." Then I walk to the opposite side of the platform and say, "Earth was all the way over here where it was." I continue to say, "Then God had an idea. As if a new thought could ever occur to the all-knowing God. But if He could have had a new idea, this would have been the idea He would have had at this moment. It would have started with Him asking Himself a question. 'How can I bring Heaven and Earth together?' His solution to the distance, and separation between Heaven and Earth would be to create man."

Man is the living, breathing manifestation of God's desire to bring Heaven and Earth together. Let me say that again because I think it's crucial to understand. The creation of man is because of God's desire to bring Heaven and Earth together in one place. To further clarify, it was to bring Heaven and Earth together in one person. That person would be His son, Adam. That's how God designed us, and our destiny is revealed in that design. Since we are designed as Heaven and Earth, our destiny is to implore Heaven to show up on the Earth by developing a prayer life and a practical life that says, "Your Kingdom come. Your will be done, on Earth as it is in Heaven."

Designed for the Supernatural

Our Destiny - Bring Heaven to Earth

Our Design - Heaven and Earth

Our design allows us to easily accomplish our destiny. Once again, we see the genius of Divine intellect at work. God would not command us to live supernaturally if He did not design us to be supernatural beings. That would be illogical and irrational. God is neither of those things. Since our destiny is to be supernatural, it makes sense that we are designed with supernatural capabilities. It is the Spirit of God within us that activates our Divine design. We see this concept of supernatural capabilities and Divine design in Matthew Chapter 6.

Matthew 6:25-33 NLT

> *"That is why I tell you not to worry about everyday life— whether you have enough food and drink, or enough clothes to wear. Isn't life more than food, and your body more than clothing?* [26] *Look at the birds. They don't plant or harvest or store food in barns, for your heavenly Father feeds them. And aren't you far more valuable to him than they are?* [27] *Can all your worries add a single moment to your life?* [28] *"And why worry about your clothing? Look at the lilies of the field and how they grow. They don't work or make their clothing,* [29] *yet Solomon in all his glory was not dressed as beautifully as they are.* [30] *And if God cares so wonderfully for wildflowers that are here today and thrown into the fire tomorrow, he will certainly care for you. Why do you have so little faith?* [31] *"So don't worry about these things, saying, 'What will we eat? What will we drink? What will we wear?'* [32] *These things dominate the thoughts of unbelievers, but your heavenly*

Father already knows all your needs. ³³Seek the Kingdom of God above all else, and live righteously, and he will give you everything you need.

I have preached from this passage of Scripture more times than I can even remember. I have preached about trusting God, faith in God, the Kingdom of God, and the trap of worrying. All of which are important messages to glean from this text. But there is one message that, whenever I preach it, people always comment on how they didn't realize that such a message could be drawn from this passage. It's about how easy God intended it to be for everyone on Earth to respond to the way He designed them. It's about how natural it is for supernatural beings to function supernaturally.

Notice that Jesus first points out the birds of the air and then draws our attention to the flowers of the field. This is not just about birds and lilies. There's a deeper point to His analogy. In essence, what Jesus was saying is, "Observe everything in creation!" When you observe nature, you'll find out that humans are the only species in God's creation that stresses themselves out, worrying about the whats, the whens, and the hows of God's plans and provisions.

Whether you're observing the birds that fly in the air or the flowers that grow from the ground, they all have one thing in common. They are God's creations. And creation does not struggle or reason with the will of the Creator; creation simply responds to the will of the Creator. Who has ever heard of the waters of the sea reasoning with God as to whether or not it was His will for it to create waves that day? No one has because it's never happened. When we stand on a beach on a stormy day, we just see wave after wave leaping from seething waters and crashing against the craggy rocks of sandy seashores.

I've never heard of a lion waking up in the middle of the jungle and asking the Creator whether or not it was His will for him to roar that day. Absolutely not! The lion just roars because that's a part of His design. He doesn't reason with it or struggle against it. *National Geographic* has never told the story of an eagle that struggled with God as to whether or not it was His will for it to ride a morning gust of wind up to a snow-capped mountaintop.

No, eagles just soar, lions just roar, flowers just grow, and the sun just rises and sets as it was created to do. Creation doesn't reason with the will of the Creator; it simply responds to it. Stop and let that sink in for a moment. Once again, creation doesn't reason with the will of the Creator; it simply responds to it. The stars don't ask the One who created them if they should shine; they just do. Because the intention of the Creator has already been revealed in their design, and they cannot help but do what He designed them to do.

God's wonderful creation never got the memo that fulfilling your purpose is supposed to be much harder than they're making it. Dogs aren't afraid of barking; cat's aren't afraid of purring; ducks aren't reluctant to quack. Snakes naturally slither, cows naturally moo, and chickens naturally cluck, all naturally functioning the way they were created to. I've never seen a dolphin that couldn't swim or a whale that was afraid of drowning. But almost every day, I meet believers who don't believe and Christians who don't know how to manifest Christ! Fulfilling God's will for your life is not supposed to be complicated. It's as easy as a shark swimming or a lion roaring. All it takes is for us to stop reasoning with our religious perspectives and start responding to our Divine design.

Spirit, Soul, and Body

One of the easiest ways that I have discovered to simplify a theological thought that people aren't readily connected to is to use illustrations and demonstrations. I love to employ such visuals when teaching about the Spirit, Soul, and Body. I do that by calling four people up to the platform to be my visual aids. Three of them represent the Spirit, Soul, and Body of a human being. The fourth person represents a man or woman who doesn't know God. I represent God (only because it's easy for me to demonstrate how God moves from the Spirit realm to the natural realm). I have the Spirit, Soul, and Body face the congregation. Together, they represent a human being. The space to their right represents Heaven. The space to the left of them represents Earth.

I (who represent God) am standing in the space that's symbolic of Heaven. The man or woman who doesn't know God is standing in the space that represents Earth. Then I say this, "God is over here, in

Heaven, wanting to get into your Earth. But His only access point into the Earth is through you. With your Body, you have access to Earth. With your Spirit, you have access to Heaven. And your Spirit and Body communicate to one another through your Soul. The Soul is the arbitrator, the go-between, the intercessor, and the bridge between your Spirit, and your body. Therefore, it's also the bridge between Heaven and Earth. The condition of your Soul determines how much of God gets to be in your world, or how much of the world will hinder your ability to experience God."

That illustration can last up to 30 minutes or more, but it is very effective. At the end of the analogy, my goal is to get the God of Heaven into the space that represents Earth. And get the man who doesn't know God to meet Him and gain access to Heaven. But it all depends on the soul. Watchman Nee refers to the soul in his book, *The Spiritual Man* as "The seat of man's individuality." He explains that the soul is comprised of the mind, will, and emotions. This is why Romans 12 impresses upon us the importance of the "renewing of your mind." As a part of the analogy, I often turn the Soul toward the Body, and away from the Spirit. I do this to illustrate the word picture of Acts 2:40. Peter, while preaching on the day of Pentecost, said, "Save yourselves from this *untoward* generation."

Untoward = Your interests, appetites, and pursuits are turned away from God and toward the world.

So, Peter was admonishing the new converts to keep themselves from a culture whose appetites, interests, and pursuits are turned away from God, and toward a self-serving world. This is what the Bible calls the flesh.

Galatians 5:17

For the flesh wars against the Spirit, and the Spirit against the flesh: and these are opposing one another: so that ye cannot do the things that you should.

When I was younger, I used to think that what the Bible calls the flesh was my body. I thought that my body was warring against my spirit. When I really studied it, I realized that was not the case at all. The flesh is not the body. The flesh is a soul whose interests, appetites, and pursuits are turned away from God and toward the world. Or toward pleasing the body. It's a soul that is far more aware of the pleasures of the physical world and not the purposes and pleasures of the spiritual world.

Colossians 3:1-2 AMP

If then you have been raised with Christ [to a new life, thus sharing His resurrection from the dead], aim at and seek the [rich, eternal treasures] that are above, where Christ is, seated at the right hand of God. ² And set your minds and keep them set on what is above (the higher things), not on the things that are on the earth.

KJV says, *"Set your affection, (soul), on things above, (heaven), and not on things of this world."*

Your affection is your earthly condition. The things above are your heavenly position. Your struggle in life is trying to get your earthly condition aligned with your heavenly position. That means that your struggle in life is trying to get your soul in tune with your spirit. There are two kinds of believers in the world:

1. The believer that's allowing their earthly condition to hinder them from experiencing their heavenly position.

2. The believer who is allowing their heavenly position to transform their earthly condition.

This transformation takes place by applying the word of God. The word of God turns the soul toward the human spirit, and empowers it to worship God. Your spirit always wants to worship God, but is oftentimes silenced by the appetites of your soul. That's where the role of God's word in man's tripartite being comes into the picture. Tripartite is just a big word for threefold. Man is a threefold being because we are spirit, soul, and body. Let's look at what the word of God does to man's threefold being.

Hebrews 4:12 NLT

For the word of God is alive and powerful. It is sharper than the sharpest two-edged sword, cutting between soul and spirit, between joint and marrow. It exposes our innermost thoughts and desires.

This text is the description of the word of God operating in man's spirit, soul, and body. The soul and spirit are mentioned first. The "joint and marrow," which is the human body, is mentioned last. These three parts are not mentioned in order of importance. It just demonstrates how the word of God operates when it enters into a human being.

When God first created man, man's human spirit was at the helm of his threefold being. Meaning that his human spirit was running the show. The human spirit was in charge of the soul, and the soul told the body what to do. So, mankind was first a spiritual being before he became an emotional and intellectual being. His intellect and emotions were under the government of his human spirit. And his human spirit was under the government of the Holy Spirit. And his body was a servant to whatever his soul wanted. So the mind will and emotions of mankind, under the government of man's human spirit, dictated to the human body what it was supposed to do. So, it was easier for Man to be governed by the Holy Spirit, because his human spirit was at the head of his existence.

However, after the fall of man, his human spirit was no longer at the head of his existence. His soul, which was once turned toward his human spirit, was now turned toward his body. And his mind, will, and emotions had now become a slave to the appetites and interests of his body. The human body that was once a servant to his spirit and soul was now the part of him calling the shots. So, when the body wants sexual pleasure, the soul says yes and grants the body whatever it wants as much as it wants. When the body craves food, the soul says yes and grants the body whatever kind of food it wants, as much as it wants. But when God's Holy Spirit enters the human spirit, the human spirit is put back in charge of the human being. It is only then that the human spirit has the strength to assert its rightful authority over the soul and the body.

So, when the word of God enters into man's threefold being, it is not only the bread that feeds him and the medicine that heals him but it's also the surgical scalpel that cuts him.

Hebrews 4:12 MSG

God means what he says. What he says goes. His powerful Word is sharp as a surgeon's scalpel, cutting through everything...

Here's how it works: God uses His Word to do surgery on your spirit and soul. His Holy Spirit awakens your sleeping spirit, and then He uses His word to divide your soul and spirit, giving you the ability to distinguish between the two. Before He did that, your spirit was asleep and powerless to stop the sinful affections and appetites of your body and soul. But now that you are spiritually awakened, God uses his word to do some internal rearranging. He puts your threefold being back in its proper order. So instead of functioning, as you did in your fallen state, from the outside in, (body, soul, and spirit), you now function in your renewed state from the inside out (spirit, soul, and body). The word of God turns the interests, appetites, and pursuits of your soul toward God, discerning and exposing your thoughts and desires, and then empowers your spirit to serve God unhindered by your soul and body.

Just as Much Access

The two primary materials that man is made up of, (the materials of Heaven and of Earth) give him easy, continual access to both the heavenly and earthly dimensions. Man's spirit is just as much spiritual as his body is physical, so his spirit should experience just as much of the spiritual realm as his body experiences the physical realm. I'm supposed to have just as much access to Heaven as I do to Earth, since my spirit is made up of just as much of the material of Heaven as my body is made up of the material of earth. Your human body is 100% physical. That means that your human body has 100% access to the physical realm. Your human spirit is 100% spiritual. That means that your human spirit is supposed to have 100% access to the spiritual realm.

Man was created both spiritual and physical. That means that man was designed to have just as much access to Heaven as he does to Earth. But somewhere along the line, our muddled theology taught us that we were only supposed to experience God occasionally. Let me ask you a question. Does your physical body experience Earth occasionally? I'm going to assume you answered no. How often does your physical man experience Earth? I'm going to assume, again that you answered, "All the time."

So, if your physical man experiences Earth all the time, how often should your spiritual man experience Heaven? You're exactly right. All the time. It's not an unusual phenomenon for your body to experience Earth. So, it shouldn't be an unusual phenomenon for your spirit to experience Heaven.

It's Literal

On a daily basis, I'm always writing down multiple revelations and amazing insights that God reveals to me. But every so often, God gives me an insight into a spiritual truth that causes a major paradigm shift in my thinking. Years ago, God revealed something to me that did just that. As I was reflecting on the many conversations I've had with people over the years about spiritual things, I realized that most of them, even the Christians, had a warped view of the spirit world. Most people view the spiritual realm as a far away, mystical, mythical, and ethereal realm instead of a very real, tangible, and literal realm. It is my opinion that what I'm about to share with you is the barrier that has prevented man from truly living in the spirit. And if we will really grasp it, it will change us forever.

Natural things reveal spiritual things, and the spiritual realm is the birthing place of the natural realm. The psychological perception of the spiritual realm is that it is mystical. Whereas the psychological perception of the physical realm is that it is literal. The spiritual realm is not a mystical realm; the spiritual realm is a literal realm. Even more so than the physical because the physical literally gets its existence from the spiritual. Because we have associated spiritual things with mystical things, we have unintentionally reduced spiritual things to figurative things.

For instance, salvation did not figuratively or symbolically seat us together in heavenly places with Jesus Christ. Salvation spiritually, literally, and actually seated us together in heavenly places with Christ Jesus. I am not figuratively in possession of the power of God. I am literally, actually, in possession of the power of God, to the degree that this spiritual power can and is intended to transform my physical world. Something doesn't have to be physical in order for it to be literal. WOW! Think on that for a minute.

Acts 3:1-8 NKJV

Now, Peter and John went up together to the temple at the hour of prayer, the ninth hour. ²And a certain man lame from his mother's womb was carried, whom they laid daily at the gate of the temple, which is called Beautiful, to ask alms from those who entered the temple; ³who, seeing Peter and John about to go into the temple, asked for alms. ⁴ And fixing his eyes on him, with John, Peter said, "Look at us." ⁵So he gave them his attention, expecting to receive something from them. ⁶Then Peter said, "Silver and gold I do not have, but what I do have I give you: In the name of Jesus Christ of Nazareth, rise up and walk." ⁷And he took him by the right hand and lifted him up, and immediately his feet and ankle bones received strength. ⁸So he, leaping up, stood and walked and entered the temple with them——walking, leaping, and praising God.

Peter didn't see the lame man and say to him, *"I don't have the power to heal you, but God does. So, I will pray for you, so that God will have mercy on you, and heal you."* Peter said, *"What I have, I give you."* The KJV says, *"Such as I have, give I thee..."* Peter wasn't figuratively in possession of the power of God. He was literally and actually in possession of God's power. Dare I say that the spiritual power of God was surging through his physical body? The reason I know that is because the Bible says of the lame man that *"...his feet and ankle bones received strength..."* Where did he receive the strength from? Did it come from Peter's prayer? No. Because Peter didn't pray for him. So, the lame man's physical body received strength from the spiritual power that was flowing through Peter's physical body. Peter was actually, tangibly, and literally in possession of the eternal merchandise of God's spiritual power. Please don't misunderstand me. God is the one who got the glory, but he gave Peter the power to perform this miracle.

If you allow me, I'd like you to try something that will help you clearly understand the point I'm making. If you carry a wallet or a pocketbook, where you keep cash, credit or debit cards, or your checkbook, pull it out as quickly as you can. If it's not nearby, briefly place this book down and go find it. As quickly as possible, get your hands on some sort of currency. Do you have it? If you do, hold it out in front of you so that you can see it really well.

Now, I want you to realize something. Just as easy as it was for you to reach for your physical currency and pull it out so that you can see it with your eyes, is as easy as it should be to reach into your spirit man and pull out the power, anointing, favor, and wisdom of God, to use it whenever you or someone else is in need of it. If I was preaching this in a worship service right now, I would put the microphone down on the podium and walk away from the pulpit while shaking my head. Or I would do something to that effect. I wouldn't be doing that because the sermon was over, but only because I'm a very intense and animated preacher, and I think this point is a very big deal that I don't want anyone to miss.

If you went shopping and saw something that you really wanted that cost $10, and you had $100 to spend on whatever you wanted, you would confidently purchase that $10 item. Because you would be in possession of more than enough money to buy it. Peter didn't have to pray that God would heal the man, because he already had a relationship with God and a prayer life that caused him to be in literal possession of more than enough spiritual power to bring physical healing to this man. As easy as it is to reach into your pocket and pull out some money, it is as easy as it was for Peter to reach into the spirit world and pull out the miracle-working power of God. And that is as easy as it should be for you and me to do the same.

Genesis 3:8 says that God would come down and walk with man in the cool of the day. God was not figuratively walking with Adam. God would literally take a walk with Adam. Adam would be physically walking, and this spiritual God would come down to walk with Adam's physical man. Consider that. This means that even your physical man was originally designed to interact with a spiritual God. It ought to be just as normal for you to be in the presence of angels, as it is for you to sit at the kitchen table with your wife and children.

Spiritual things have become extraordinary to us when they are supposed to be ordinary, and the lack of the supernatural is supposed to be unusual. The supernatural power of God has to once again become normal to the believer. Seeing God ought to be just as normal as it is to wake up, open your eyes, and see your spouse in the bed next to you.

Overhearing

Whenever I am finished preaching a sermon or just leaving a worship service, I am absolutely restless. I have all kinds of revelations bouncing around in my head. My wife becomes a captive audience of one to my revelatory rantings. Sometimes, it's just excitement and my mind racing before I wind down for the night. At other times, it's the Spirit of the Lord revealing things to me that I need to pay attention to. There was one such occasion, in my early twenties, when I had an experience that caused me to understand seeing into the spirit realm and hearing God's voice in a different way.

I had returned home to Atlanta, Georgia, from preaching a three-night crusade in Columbus, Ohio. I had not slept in two days because of the abundance of revelations, I was receiving. It was incredible but overwhelming. After I sat down on the couch to unwind before I went to bed, the force of divine insight became stronger. I was grateful that God was speaking to me about so many things, but I couldn't physically handle it anymore. I prayed. "God, I just want to go to sleep. Please stop speaking to me for now. Let's start again tomorrow." I figured that was a reasonable enough request for God to understand. Immediately, I heard God respond, "I am not speaking to you."

I was stunned to hear that. After all, I was receiving the most fantastic insights about God and His Kingdom. Now God is telling me that this whole time, He's not the one talking to me. So I figured maybe God was being technical. So I prayed again, "Lord, please stop showing me these things, and let's resume again tomorrow. I really have to sleep." He immediately responded again. "I'm not showing you anything." I jumped to my feet with every hair on my body standing at attention." "What do you mean you're not the one speaking to me, or showing me things?" I exclaimed. Then it hit me like a Mack truck. God said, "You're living in my house. And just as a toddler, at his father's feet, overhears his father's conversations, you're overhearing the things that are being said, and you're seeing the activities that are transpiring."

Needless to say, I stayed up the rest of the night writing more revelations. But I think I slept at least 11 hours the following day. That's extremely long for someone who sleeps, five to six hours on average.

I learned that not everything you hear God say is something He is necessarily saying to you. But He allows you to hear it because you're His child, you're living in His house, and you're sitting at His feet.

Jesus, the Best of Both Worlds

Remember that God came to Earth as a man to show us the man that He desired all men to be. That's why He is Jesus Christ.

Jesus - *Man*

Christ - *God*

He's the best of both worlds. God and man coexisting in the same environment.

Jesus - *Earth*

Christ - *Heaven*

Jesus Christ is Heaven and Earth harmoniously living together under the same roof. God created man to unite Heaven and Earth, by binding both worlds together in the man. So whenever the man did something pertaining to Heaven, he took Earth with him. When he did something pertaining to Earth, he took Heaven with him. When he was drinking water from a fresh spring, Heaven was with him. When he was peering beyond the balcony of eternity, at choirs of angels gathering before the throne, Earth was with him.

So when man fell into sin, his heavenly aspect was also affected. He was still designed as both worlds. But he was no longer the best of those worlds. His heavenly and earthly nature was now defective and diminished. So, God became a man in order to stage the ultimate reunion. He became a man not only to reunite God and man but also to reunite Heaven and Earth together in the body of the perfect man. He became what He initially created us to be. The best of both worlds. That's why when he resurrected from the dead, he said, *"All power is given to me in Heaven and in Earth."* Because he legally united both realms together. The reason that God designed us as Heaven and Earth, is because, when Heaven and Earth are in the same place, He is always with us, and we are always with Him. That was the design in the beginning and that will be our destiny in the end.

CHAPTER 8
A PRIESTLY KINGDOM

We are not the best of both worlds just so that we can have access to both worlds. We are the best of both worlds so that we can give God access to our Earth and give men access to God's Heaven. Because of this, we function as biblical priests, and prophets who "stand in the gap" for the world. If I were doing an exhaustive teaching on the priesthood, I would spend a considerable amount of time showing you how Christ is a priest after the order of Melchizedek. And I would also delve headlong into the rich symbolism of the Levitical Priesthood. But I'm not doing an in-depth teaching on the priesthood. I'm rather focusing our attention on the aspect of priestly ministry that caused them to stand between two worlds and how that pertains to us. In this chapter, we're going to focus on what it means to be a priestly person as it relates to the best of both worlds. It's some pretty good stuff, so let's get into it.

What is a Priest?

Maybe what comes to your mind when I say the word priesthood, is the pomp and ceremony of Roman Catholicism. So, when I talk about the Priestly Kingdom, you immediately think about rosary beads, Sunday morning mass, communion wine and confessional booths. But that is the furthest thing from my mind when I refer to this misunderstood and yet vitally essential ministry. What comes to mind is a New Testament scripture that puts the priesthood in a perspective that applies to every believer in a very practical way.

Hebrews 5:1-5 NLT

Every High Priest is a man chosen to represent other people in their dealings with God. He presents their gifts to God and offers sacrifices for their sins. ²And he is able to deal gently with ignorant and wayward people because he himself is subject to the same weaknesses. ³That is why he must offer sacrifices for his own sins as well as theirs. ⁴And no one can become a High Priest simply because he wants such an honor. He must be called by God for this work, just as Aaron was. ⁵That is why Christ did not honor himself by assuming he could become High Priest. No, he was chosen by God, who said to him, "You are my Son. Today I have become your Father."

A priest is a man taken from among men to represent the interests of the people in the presence of God. He offers gifts and sacrifices to God on behalf of the people. But there was also someone known as the High Priest. This is what Aaron, the brother of Moses, was. The High Priest was the leader of all of the priests and the religious leader of the people. Every year, on the Day of Atonement, he alone was allowed to enter behind the veil of the Tabernacle of Moses, in the Holy of Holies, to stand in the Presence of God. After making a sacrifice for himself and the people, he then brought the blood into the Holy of Holies and sprinkled it on the mercy seat, which they also called, the throne of God. Leviticus 16:14-15. This was symbolic of what Jesus, our Great High Priest would do thousands of years later.

Our Great High Priest

Hebrews 4:14-16 NLT

So then, since we have a great High Priest who has entered heaven, Jesus the Son of God, let us hold firmly to what we believe. ¹⁵ This High Priest of ours understands our weaknesses, for he faced all of the same testing we do, yet he did not sin. ¹⁶So, let us come boldly to the throne of our gracious God. There we will receive his mercy, and we will find grace to help us when we need it most.

This passage references Christ's priestly ministry. As our Great High Priest, He ascended and entered into Heaven. We teach the death, burial, and resurrection of Jesus. But most of us do not teach, or even understand the doctrine of the ascension. Christ's redemptive work was not complete until He ascended into Heaven.

Ephesians 4:7-10

He climbed the high mountain, He captured the enemy and seized the spoils, He handed it all out in gifts to the people. Is it not true that the One who climbed up also climbed down, down to the valley of earth? And the One who climbed down is the One who climbed back up, up to highest heaven. He handed out gifts above and below, filled heaven with his gifts, filled earth with his gifts.

Hebrews 7:23-25 VOICE

Further, the prior priesthood of the sons of Levi has included many priests because death cut short their service, 24 but Jesus holds His priesthood permanently because He lives His resurrected life forever. 25 From such a vantage, He is able to save those who approach God through Him for all time because He will forever live to be their advocate in the presence of God.

What a triumphant picture these passages of Scripture paint for us. Most people don't even realize that Jesus did all of this in His incarnation and ascension. This passage does not refer to a suffering servant nailed to a dreadful tree. It refers to a time when an Alien King from an ageless world devised a masterful plot to rescue the human race from its foreseeable demise. After bullying death in the belly of hell, He restored life to fallen man and made those who believed in Him a brand-new race. Then He distributed the eternal spoils of His warfare throughout the galaxies of the universe and climbed back up into the mountain of eternity, where He awaits His final and most epic invasion of human history. Until then, He has secured a seat of authority for His rescued race at the right hand of the Father. That seat is the very throne on which He sits to intercede for them.

We must understand that without the ascension of our resurrected Alien King, humanity does not have adequate representation in Heaven. Without Jesus ascending into the throne room of Heaven and sprinkling His blood on the mercy seat, the act of redemption is not finalized, and humanity has no heavenly representation. It doesn't matter if we are designed to be the best of both worlds; if Jesus never ascended into

Heaven; we would never be authorized to access His world. When He resurrected, we inherited His life. When He ascended, we inherited His throne. Wow! What a big statement! I assure you it's in no way blasphemous. It's entirely biblical.

Ephesians 2:6-7 NLT

For he raised us from the dead along with Christ and seated us with him in the heavenly realms because we are united with Christ Jesus. ⁷ So God can point to us in all future ages as examples of the incredible wealth of his grace and kindness toward us, as shown in all he has done for us who are united with Christ Jesus.

1. "He raised us from the dead along with Christ" - The resurrection of Christ was so that a new race could be revived with Him.

2. "Seated us with him in the heavenly realms" - The ascension of Christ was so that the race that revived with Him could rule with Him.

The resurrection is about reviving in newness of life, but the ascension is about ruling and reigning with Christ. We don't have to wait till we get to Heaven to access it; we can start accessing it right now. That's what the priestly ministry of Jesus is all about. It's about us realizing that if we died with Him and resurrected with Him, then we also ascended with Him! And because of that, we are positioned spiritually with Him right now. That means that we have access to everything that Jesus in Heaven has access to because our Great High Priest is in Heaven working on our behalf.

The Bridge to Heaven

A prophet is a person sent from God to represent the interests of God in the presence of people. A priest, on the other hand, is a person taken from among people to represent the interests of the people in the presence of God.

The prophet faces the people representing God. The priest faces God representing the people. Every time I explain this to people, they understand the priest and prophet in a way they didn't understand it before. The priest wasn't some mysterious Old Testament figure, too holy for us to understand him. He is a picture of what God became as a man and what He intends all of us to be. He is the bridge between two realms.

"So let us come boldly to the throne." Why are we able to approach the Throne of God with confidence?

The reason is because what Jesus, our Great High Priest, did in His ascension gave us legal access to the throne room of God. As I said earlier, everything Jesus did, He didn't just do it for us; He did it as us. He didn't just live for us; He lived as us. Jesus didn't just die for humanity on the cross; He died as humanity on the cross. He didn't just resurrect for humanity from the grave; He resurrected as humanity from the grave. He didn't just ascend for humanity into Heaven; He ascended as humanity into Heaven!

So because of that, you and I have the authorization to enter into the throne room of God with the assurance that we have the legal right to be there! Because in Christ, we already are there. Heaven is not just our future home; it's our present home. We won't just go there someday; in a sense, we are there today if we're in Christ! Our spirit is created for Heaven and our bodies are created for earth. So, our home is Heaven on Earth. It's all because Jesus is our Great High Priest! He is our intercessor and our bridge from Earth to Heaven. He is us in the Presence of God, and we are Him in the presence of men. He is us in Heaven, and we are Him in the earth. WOW! Hallelujah!!

Remember the 'the-anthropological revolution' I talked about before? Well, this is it: God in Earth, and man in Heaven. What is the practical application of that? I'm glad you asked. Most Christians have some understanding of the fact that Jesus is our Great High Priest, and He functions as our bridge to Heaven. What most Christians don't realize is that we, as God's children, are a part of a Priestly Kingdom, and we are supposed to function as the world's bridge to Heaven. Let me say that again.

Most Christians have some understanding of the fact that Jesus is our Great High Priest, and He functions as our bridge to Heaven. What most Christians don't realize is that we, as God's children, are a part of a

Priestly Kingdom, and we are supposed to function as the world's bridge to Heaven.

1 Peter 2:9, NLT

…You are royal priests, a holy nation, God's very own possession. As a result, you can show others the goodness of God, for He called you out of the darkness into his wonderful light.

No one can get to Heaven by believing in the Church, but the Church's role in the world is to bridge the gap between God and man by showing others the goodness of God. The reason the Church can always be confident about approaching the throne for help is because Jesus is always interceding for us in God's presence. He is fulfilling His intercessory role on our behalf. The reason the world can't always be confident about approaching the Church for help is because we are not always interceding for the world in the presence of God. We are not fulfilling our intercessory role on their behalf. He is doing a great job of being us in the presence of the Father. Because of that, we always have access to His world. The modern Church is doing a terrible job of being Him in the presence of our family and friends; because of that, He seldom has access to our world, and the world seldom has access to Him.

Romans 8:34 NLT

"…Christ Jesus died for us and was raised to life for us, and he is sitting in the place of honor at God's right hand, pleading for us."

This is a picture of Christ's priestly, intercessory ministry for the Church. It's also a picture of the Church's Priestly, intercessory ministry for the world.

1 John 4:16-17 NLT

We know how much God loves us, and we have put our trust in his love. God is love, and all who live in love live in God, and God lives in them. [17] And as we live in God, our love grows more perfect. So we will not be afraid on the day of judgment, but we can face him with confidence because we live like Jesus here in this world.

There is so much to unpack in this passage of scripture. Notice that this scripture is not in the past tense; it's in the present tense. It doesn't say, "We live like Jesus lived when He was in this world." It says, "We live like Jesus here in this world." It's not referring to the past; it's referring to the present. As a matter of fact, the KJV says, *"As He is, so are we in this world."* It doesn't say, "How He was when He was on Earth." It says, "As He is." The inference is that how Jesus is presently positioned in Heaven, is how God has presently positioned us in the Earth.

Let me ask you a question. How is Jesus in Heaven? What is His role and function there? Let me answer that question for you. His current role is Intercessor, Go-between, and Bridge to Heaven. His function is ruling, reigning, and interceding for the Believer. That's how He is in Heaven, and that's how we ought to be in the Earth. We're in the world as an extension of the rule and reign of Christ, interceding for humanity in the throne room of God!

2 Corinthians 5:17-20 NLT

This means that anyone who belongs to Christ has become a new person. The old life is gone; a new life has begun![18] *And all of this is a gift from God, who brought us back to himself through Christ. And God has given us the task of reconciling people to him.* [19] *For God was in Christ, reconciling the world to himself, no longer counting people's sins against them. And he gave us this wonderful message of reconciliation.* [20] *So we are Christ's ambassadors; God is making his appeal through us. We speak for Christ when we plead, "Come back to God!"*

Jesus' responsibility in Heaven is to intercede for His Church. Our responsibility on Earth is to intercede for the world. All of our words and ways should be a bridge to the door of the Kingdom of God.

Stairway to Heaven

The 1971 classic, "Stairway to Heaven," by English rock band Led Zeppelin has broken all kinds of records. It's hailed as one of the greatest rock songs of all time. The stairway the legendary rock band was singing about so many years ago doesn't lead to the Heaven of the Bible. But the Bible does talk about a real stairway to Heaven. Speaking of the great third-generation patriarch, Jacob:

Genesis 28:11-19 NLT

At sundown he arrived at a good place to set up camp and stopped there for the night. Jacob found a stone to rest his head against and lay down to sleep. [12] As he slept, he dreamed of a stairway that reached from the earth up to heaven. And he saw the angels of God ascending and descending on the stairway. [13] At the top of the stairway stood the Lord, and he said, "I am the Lord, the God of your grandfather Abraham, and the God of your father, Isaac. The ground you are lying on belongs to you. I am giving it to you and your descendants. [14] Your descendants will be as numerous as the dust of the earth! They will spread out in all directions—to the west and the east, to the north and the south. And all the families of the earth will be blessed through you and your descendants. [15] What's more, I am with you, and I will protect you wherever you go. One day I will bring you back to this land. I will not leave you until I have finished giving you everything I have promised you." [16] Then Jacob awoke from his sleep and said, "Surely the Lord is in this place, and I wasn't even aware of it!" [17] But he was also afraid and said, "What an awesome place this is! It is none other than the house of God, the very gateway to heaven!" [18] The next morning Jacob got up very early. He took the stone he had rested his head against, and he set it upright as a memorial pillar. Then he poured olive oil over it. [19] He named that place Bethel (which means "house of God").

Let's fast forward, for a moment, thousands of years later, to when Jesus undoubtedly makes reference to Jacob's experience.

John 1:51 NLT

Then he said, "I tell you the truth, you will all see heaven open and the angels of God going up and down on the Son of Man, the one who is the stairway between heaven and earth."

Here, Jesus reveals that He is the stairway of Jacob. What He was saying is, "I am the portal through which mankind will have re- entry into the heavenly dimensions he lost access to."

That's awesome!!! But remember that Jesus is not just our Savior, He is also our example. And we are an extension of what He is. That means that as His body on the Earth, we are the world's Stairway to Heaven. So, the Church and Body of Christ is the portal through which mankind will re-enter into the heavenly dimensions it lost access to in the Garden of Eden. There are souls that will only find their way to God because of your willingness to be their Stairway to Heaven.

I believe that Jacob heard his father Isaac, and his grandfather Abraham, talk about the power, glory, and promise of God for their descendants. I also believe that until Jacob had this supernatural encounter for himself, he didn't realize the heavenly dimensions that were available to him, his descendants, and humanity in general. I believe that this experience revolutionized Jacob's perspective of the relationship between God and man and Heaven and Earth.

From Adam's fall to this stairway to heaven encounter, the general consensus of people concerning God, was that He was the Holy Judge of the universe, seated on a heavenly throne. But I believe that after this experience Jacob realized that God didn't just want man to be on Earth, while He stays in Heaven. What He really wants is for the two worlds to interact with one another. That is what God has always wanted. I am convinced that He has always desired for there to be an overlapping of Heaven and Earth.

Whenever I'm driving out of state, I always depend on my trusty GPS to guide me safely to my destination. It's very dependable, most of the time. My wife is just as good, or better than the GPS because I always tease her that she has a state-of-the-art GPS built into her brain. She, like my older sister Trudy, has an incredible sense of direction, and knows her way around a steering wheel. Even though I used to drive trucks for a living, I, on the other hand, am directionally challenged. But I love to drive. Go figure.

There's nothing like the open road, a smartphone to record one's thoughts, a sleeping wife in the passenger seat next to you, and sleeping kids in the back seat to keep you company. They all fall asleep as soon as we pull out of the driveway. It's adorable.

I really enjoy those road trips. I get to drive and record my thoughts as they come to me. If we're on our way from West Palm Beach, Florida (where my dad lives), and heading back to Georgia, he'll call me and ask, "So where are you guys now?" Or if we're coming from Memphis,

Tennessee (where Sheretha's family lives), her dad will call us with the same question.

On one particular road trip, I was on the phone with my father, and I told him, "I think we're pretty close to Georgia. We'll probably get there any minute now." Sheretha, who I thought was sound asleep, said, "We've actually been in Georgia for 10 minutes." "Are you sure?" I asked her. With her eyes still closed and her seat reclined (sounding as if she was between sleep and wake), she responded, "I think so." She was absolutely right! We were in Georgia.

I left one state and entered into a completely different state without even realizing it. A few minutes later, it occurred to me, "This is what happened to Jacob in Genesis 28." It sent me on a train of thought that blew my mind. How many times do you fly on airplanes without realizing how many different cities, states, and countries you pass through? Unless you're looking out of the window, or the captain or a flight attendant brings it to your attention, you have no way of knowing exactly where you are. Yet you're still traveling through places you're unaware of. If it's possible to travel through cities, states, and countries without realizing it, then it must be possible to journey in and out of spiritual territory without realizing it, either!

The Bible says that it's possible to entertain angels and be unaware of it. If it's possible to be in the presence of angelic beings from Heaven, while living on Earth, without realizing it, then isn't it also possible to enter into spiritual territory and dimensions of God's glory without recognizing it? Of course it is. Because the Kingdom of God (spiritual and physical) all belong to God, and He designed us to experience all of it. It was Jesus who said, *"It is the Father's good pleasure to give you the Kingdom."* (Luke 12:32) Just as we don't always notice when we physically cross a city limit or a state line, I believe God intended for it to be the same with Heaven and Earth. It should be normal for Him to experience our Earth and for us to experience His Heaven. It is normal, in fact, that we don't always notice exactly when we transition out of one and into the other.

A.L.I.E.N.S.

2 Corinthians 12:2-4 NLT

I was caught up to the third heaven fourteen years ago. Whether I was in my body or out of my body, I don't know - only God knows. ³Yes, only God knows whether I was in my body or outside my body. But I do know ⁴that I was caught up to paradise and heard things so astounding that they cannot be expressed in words, things no human is allowed to tell.

Paul had a major spiritual experience in the Third Heaven. This spiritual experience felt so tangible to him that he couldn't distinguish between his physical body and his spiritual man. In so much that he questions whether or not his physical body was also in that heavenly place having that spiritual experience. In this heavenly encounter, Paul's earthly body was indistinguishable to him from his spirit man. I find that extremely fascinating! Because it speaks to me of how God designed the worlds to overlap one another.

Ascending and Descending, Importing and Exporting

The descending angles are symbolic of God, who came down to be where man is. The ascending angels are symbolic of man, who, because God came down, can now go up to be where God is.

Genesis 3:8 NLT

"When the cool evening breezes were blowing, the man and his wife heard the Lord God walking about in the garden..."

Revelation 4:1 NLT

"Then as I looked, I saw a door standing open in heaven, and the same voice I had heard before spoke to me like a trumpet blast. The voice said, "Come up here, and I will show you what must happen after this."

In the first book of the Bible, God comes down to Earth to be with man. In the last book of the Bible, man goes up to Heaven to be with God. The intention of God is not for us to be able to only do either or; it was always for us to be able to do both. The Bible begins with God coming down to Earth, and ends with man going up to Heaven. Both accounts reflect the same thing. God coming down to Earth and walking with man in Genesis is God's desire to live in man's house. Man going up to Heaven in Revelation, is man's desire to live in God's house. God desires to be where we are, and we desire to be where He is. This is also symbolic of man's ability to go back and forth throughout the economy of God's Kingdom. We were created to go back and forth, traveling through the vast domain of God's spiritual and physical creation.

John 10:9 AMP

I am the Door; anyone who enters in through Me will be saved (will live). He will come in and he will go out [freely], and will find pasture.

Jesus calls Himself the Door into the Kingdom of God. Meaning that He is the gateway into every dimension of the Kingdom of God. Our relationship with Jesus Christ activates our ability to travel the immeasurable real estate of His majesty and explore the hidden treasures of His creation! God designed us to go back and forth and in and out of various dimensions and arenas of His Kingdom. After Jesus' resurrection He traveled back and forth from Earth to Heaven several times. When we receive our glorified bodies, we will be able to do the same thing. But we don't have to wait till then to experience some degree of this. For when we were born from above, our eternal life began at that moment.

At the very moment of spiritual birth, you and I entered into the Kingdom of God through the gateway of Jesus Christ and our ability to go in and out to find spiritual merchandise and provision began. The stairway represents what God always intended man to be; Heaven's connection to Earth, and Earth's connection to Heaven. It's not just a type of Christ; It's also a type of the Body of Christ. Christ is not just the head. He is His Head and His Body together. The Bible says that the top of the stairway reached Heaven, and it was from the Earth. It was connected to Heaven and Earth. Divinity and humanity. A picture of Jesus Christ.

The Top of the Ladder Reached Heaven = *Head*

The Bottom of the Ladder Came from Earth = *Body*

A.L.I.E.N.S.

Hebrews 1:7 AMP

"Referring to the angels He says, [God] Who makes His angels winds and His ministering servants flames of fire."

The word Angel means messenger. Consider that the angels descending and ascending this stairway are also emblematic of God's fiery messengers who will be urgently trafficking in and out of Heavenly realms, importing and exporting valuable spiritual commodities. They represent every messenger of God's Kingdom, who burns with Heavenly fire to transport the treasures of eternity to the ends of the Earth and transport the burdens of men into the throne room of God.

I Wasn't Aware of It

Jacob woke up from his dream, and said, "Surely the Lord is in this place, and I wasn't even aware of it!" This seems like such a strange thing for Jacob to say. For certain he knew that God was in every place and could show up at any place. So why was he so astonished about the presence of God being there? Or was that really what was astonishing to him? The two English words, translated and I, in verse 16 of Genesis 28, is translated from one Hebrew word. It's the word "anokiy" pronounced aw-no-kee.' It means, very simply, I, me, or myself. On the surface, this doesn't seem noteworthy at all. But when you study the context of this passage, it reveals something absolutely mind-blowing.

In the biblical Hebrew language, there were no punctuations, such as commas and periods. You had to pay attention to the context to determine where one thought ended and another began. When I read the context of this passage, I don't believe Jacob was saying, "I didn't know that God could be in this place." When we change where we put the punctuation, the meaning changes, and the text makes more sense. He actually said, "Yahweh was in this place and I." I believe that this was one thought all by itself. And then he continued with another thought: Yada Lo. Yada means to know, and Lo means not.

I believe what Jacob was really saying, in essence, was, "God and I were in the same place, together! I never knew or even fathomed that such a thing was possible!"

Now you understand why Jacob was so taken aback. Because there was a oneness, and union, in his dream, between him and God, that shook him to his core. "Surely God was in this place, and so was I. Heaven and Earth were in the same place together; OMG!!! I didn't know that was possible!"

Essentially, Jacob was saying, I didn't know that it was possible for God and man to co-exist in the same environment. I didn't know that I was created to have just as much access to Heaven as I do to Earth. I didn't know that God created me to be the best of both worlds!" Do you see it? Isn't that incredible?

Whichever way you put it, Jacob was blown away by the fact that Heaven and Earth were right next door to each other. And he got to experience them both at the same time, live and in color!

Gates to Glory

Verse 17 says, *"But he was also afraid and said, "What an awesome place this is! It is none other than the house of God, the very gateway to heaven!"* Verse 19 says, *"He named that place Bethel, which means "house of God."* As I began to meditate on this scripture, what the Lord revealed to me about it absolutely blew my mind. I asked myself the question, "What place was Jacob referring to?" Was he referring to the place where he had just laid down to sleep, or was he referring to something else? It's my opinion that he was referring to something else. It's actually my opinion that his statement had a double meaning. I can compare it to the Tabernacle of Moses. Though it was extremely significant, it wasn't nearly as significant as the heavenly Tabernacle it represented.

Hebrews 8:5 NLT

They serve in a system of worship that is only a copy, a shadow of the real one in heaven.

I believe that just as the Tabernacle of Moses represented something greater than itself, the physical place around Jacob was symbolic of another place that had an even greater meaning. What place was that? I believe that the place Jacob was referring to was himself. I believe that Jacob became frighteningly aware of human beings' potential to simultaneously live in the realm of Heaven and the realm of Earth at the same time. When he called the place the house of God, he wasn't just naming the city; he was identifying his body. At that moment, Jacob realized something that he spent his entire life unaware of. That is, the human body was created to be a house in which God could live in. Up to that point in history, mankind knew that God could occasionally visit Earth and then go back home to Heaven. This encounter caused Jacob to have a theological paradigm shift. Jacob realized that God created the human body to give Himself a permanent residence on the Earth. This realization terrified him. This is why Paul says in 1 Corinthians 6:19, *"Don't you realize that your body is the Temple of the Holy Spirit. Who lives in you and was given to you by God."*

Jacob was so blown away by this because the word of God passed down to him by oral tradition, talked about God coming down to Earth to occasionally visit man. It never talked about God coming down to Earth to permanently live in man. For the first time, he realizes that man's very being is a gate to the glory of God. This was an insight for which he had no mental point of reference. My take on this is not at all a clever spin on the scriptures.

John 2:19-22 NLT

"All right," Jesus replied. "Destroy this temple, and in three days I will raise it up."[20] "What!" they exclaimed. "It has taken forty-six years to build this Temple, and you can rebuild it in three days?"[21] But when Jesus said, "this temple," he meant his own body.[22] After he was raised from the dead, his disciples remembered he had said this, and they believed both the Scriptures and what Jesus had said.

Jesus was talking to them about His living body, and they thought that He was talking about a religious building. How long have we been applying to our religious buildings the things that God has been saying about His living body? How long have we expected God to bring revival to our buildings when He has been talking to us about bringing revival to His body? How long have we been waiting for God to show up in a place when He has been waiting to show up in a people?

"...they believed both the Scriptures and what Jesus had said."

The Scriptures - *the written word.*

What Jesus said - *the revealed word.*

The reason we don't understand the Scriptures is because we're not reading the scriptures in light of what Jesus has said. We're not reading the written word in light of the revealed word. What's interesting to me is that when Jesus told them to "destroy this temple," they thought he was referring to the physical temple of worship when he was actually referring to the temple of his body. It wasn't until after Jesus' resurrection that they realized what he actually meant was not the destruction of a religious building but actually the destruction of his physical body. And also the resurrection of the physical body that was destroyed. He was prophesying to them about something that was going to happen to him, and they didn't even realize it was a prophecy. So, they attributed it to something natural because they did not have the spiritual ears to understand what he was really talking about. It bothers me to no end that there are so many pastors, preachers, and church leaders today, preaching God's word after having interpreted it through the same religious and carnal perspective of those who heard Jesus talk about destroying the temple. We have built entire doctrines and even denominations on the premise of Scriptures we've misinterpreted, because we won't interpret the written word in light of the revealed word.

I hope, with all my heart, that as you're reading this book, you realize that your very being is a gateway into heavenly realms where the unsearchable riches of Christ reside. I hope that you're frighteningly aware of the fact that you are a bridge between Heaven and Earth.

After God revealed this to me from this passage, He spoke to my heart and said,

"I'm looking for gateways that will give Heaven access to earth, and earth access to Heaven." He then said to me, "I'm looking for people to give up their religious titles and prestigious positions in order to become gates into the glory of God."

If you are a pastor, you need to stop seeing yourself as a pastor alone and start seeing yourself as a gateway for your congregation to gain access to Heaven and for God to gain access to your congregation. If you're a husband or a wife, you need to start seeing yourself as a gateway for your spouse to gain access to Heaven through God's love in you for them. If you're a parent, you need to start seeing yourself as a gateway for your children to gain access to Heaven. On your job, you're not just an employee; you're a gateway for your co-workers, employees, and your employer to gain access to the presence of God within you. I don't want to be a great preacher; I want to be a great gateway for the people who know me to come into the Presence of God.

A Kingdom of Priests

Revelation 1:5-6 NLT

... Jesus Christ. He is the faithful witness to these things, the first to rise from the dead, and the ruler of all the kings of the world. All glory to him who loves us and has freed us from our sins by shedding his blood for us. [6] *He has made us a Kingdom of priests for God his Father ...*

We are a Kingdom of Priests. What does that mean? Remember what the priest does. The priest faces God in order to represent the interests of the people in the Presence of God. So, a kingdom of priests is a governing body of people who give heaven access to Earth and Earth access to Heaven. It's a Kingdom of people who bridge the gap between Heaven and Earth. It's an Empire of intercessors. It's a society whose citizens are the best of both worlds.

Hosea 4:6 NIV

My people are destroyed from lack of knowledge. "Because you have rejected knowledge, I also reject you as my priests; because you have ignored the law of your God, I also will ignore your children.

The NLT says,

"My people are being destroyed because they don't know me. Since your priests refuse to know me, I refuse to recognize you as my priests. Since you have forgotten the laws of your God, I will forget to bless your children."

We're confused between having an intellectual knowledge of God and having an intimate knowledge of God. God's people don't perish because of the lack of intellectual knowledge. They perish because of their lack of intimacy with God. Most of us know about Him, but we don't really know Him. We are a Priestly Kingdom. But before we are eligible to intercede for them, we must first be intimate with Him. For it is intimacy with God in prayer that anoints us for such intercession. After all, we don't love the people we are interceding for like God does. So, He is the only one qualified to share His heart for them with us, when we come to Him in prayer. Before the Priest went to God on the people's behalf, he went to God on his own behalf so that God could qualify him to intercede for the people. And we must do the same.

"Since your priests refuse to know me, I refuse to recognize you as my priests. Since you have forgotten the laws of your God, I will forget to bless your children."

This is how central intimacy with God is to our priestly purpose. Without it, we cannot intercede for a world that doesn't know God. Without it, we are still designed as the best of both worlds, but we will fail to bridge the gap between God and man. So, our Divine design is of no benefit to us or anyone else without a true closeness and daily fellowship with God. When we refuse this kind of intimacy with God, He refuses to recognize us as His designated chosen people to bridge the gap between the two realms. And He withdraws His hand of blessing from the generations that are born out of our prayerlessness. But when we seek to know Him, we will function as a Priestly Kingdom, interceding for the world around us. They won't have to come into a dark booth and confess their sins to an elite group of holy men. We are not their Savior. We are only a bridge to the God they have not met and a Heaven they do not know.

Awakening the Priests

Genesis 28:16-17 NLT

[16] Then Jacob awoke from his sleep and said, "Surely the Lord is in this place, and I wasn't even aware of it!" [17] But he was also afraid and said, "What an awesome place this is! It is none other than the house of God, the very gateway to heaven!"

I see Jacob making this statement after he awakened, as symbolic of a generation awakening to the astonishing revelation that God created them to be the gateway for the inhabitants of the Earth to have access to Heaven! When a generation is awakened to its Divine design, as the bridge between two worlds, that generation will become the gateway to Heaven. Standing in their presence will be like standing at the threshold of Heaven itself. I believe that we are in such a time for an awakening such as this. Where God's people realize that we are a chosen people, not anointed to go to Church but to be the Church and stand in the gap for the nations of the world. I sense that it is so. I really do. We have been slumbering in the comforts of blissful ignorance, unaware of our Priestly and prophetic purpose. Oblivious to our role in this world. But there is an awakening of divine intimacy and Priestly intercession upon us. When we truly function as a Priestly Kingdom, the world will say of the Church, "What an awesome place this is. It is none other than the house of God. The very gateway to Heaven!"

FAITH IS KNOWING THAT GOD HAS GIVEN YOU THE ABILITY TO DO THE IMPOSSIBLE.

CHAPTER 9
THE REAL YOU

God and Goobers

You can search through all the Scriptures and obtain astounding insights concerning a plethora of theological mysteries. But if you don't find yourself in its pages and understand who you are, all of your discoveries will be of no benefit to you.

We will never understand how to function in God's Kingdom until we know who we are to the King. Our Heavenly Father not only wants us to know that we are His children. He wants us to know which child we are in His house. We are not just special because we are God's children. We are special because of the specific child He made each one of us to be.

I don't go out of my way to see every superhero movie that hits the big screen. But a Superman movie is certainly not to be missed. Needless to say, my wife Sheretha and I went to the movies and saw *Man of Steel* back in 2013. We bought a large tub of popcorn, a large Sprite, and two boxes of Goobers. Only because Goobers are not to be shared. Or should I say, my Goobers are not to be shared. My wife begs to differ with that, by the way. So, when I was finished with mine, I moved on to hers. As good husbands often do.

My favorite part of the movie was when Clark and his dad were standing in front of the spaceship that brought him to Earth. "We found you in this." Mr. Kent said to his 16-year-old alien son. "We were sure the government was going to show up at our doorstep, but no one ever came." Pulling a small black metal-like object out of a wooden box he took from a dusty drawer, he gave it to Clark and said, "This was in the chamber with you. I gave it to a metallurgist at Kansas State."

"He said that whatever it was made from didn't even exist on the periodic table. Clark, that's another way of saying that it's not from this world. And neither are you. You're the answer, son. You're the answer to, 'Are we alone in the universe?'"

Clark looked back at his dad, startled, confused, and overwhelmed with all he was hearing. "I don't want to be!" He said. "And I don't blame you son. It would be a huge burden for anyone to bear. But you're not just anyone, Clark. And I have to believe that you were sent here for a reason. You're going through all these changes, and one day, you're going to think of them as a blessing. And when that day comes, you're going to have to make a choice. A choice of whether to stand proud in front of the human race or not."

The next words Clark uttered would break any father's heart. "Can't I just keep pretending I'm your son?" His dad pulled him close, embraced him, and said, "You are my son. But somewhere out there, you have another father, too, who gave you another name, and he sent you here for a reason, Clark. And even if it takes you the rest of your life, you owe it to yourself to find out what that reason is."

Sitting in that movie theater, stuffing my face with delicious buttery popcorn and mouthwatering Goobers, I could hardly contain myself. Not because of the popcorn or the Goobers, but because I was certain everyone else in the theater heard Kevin Costner, who played the role of Superman's father, speak words that solely related to the context of this fictional movie. I, on the other hand, heard him preaching spiritual truth that was blowing my mind. I immediately took out my phone and started jotting down some of the revelatory insights that kept me up the rest of that night. What I'm getting ready to share with you are the truths that have radically changed my life over the years. If you take the time to read the rest of the words that are in this book, I'm certain it has the potential to change your life as well.

What is Your Name

What is your name? Not your earthly name. What's your heavenly name?

Do you know it? The way that every child learns their name is their parents keep calling them by that name until they answer to it. The way that you learn your heavenly name is the same way. You learn it by listening to what your Heavenly Father is calling you and responding to it. The words of Clark Kent's father from *Man of Steel* should resound within all of us. "You have another father, who gave you another name, and he sent you here for a reason." When you were born into this world, your parents gave you a name. They called you by it, and eventually, you responded to what they called you.

You identify yourself by that name. It distinguishes you from everyone else. Your name sanctifies you from the rest. You are not just anyone. You are someone. If you are John Smith, you are not the same as every other John Smith on the planet. Because you are John Smith Senior or Junior. Or John Smith, the quarterback of your high school football team. The specific family, town, and time that you were born into, along with all of your personal experiences, differentiates you from every other John Smith that has ever lived and will ever live. John Smith is a common name, but you are not a common individual.

If my earthly parents gave me an earthly name that is meant to identify and distinguish me in this world; then shouldn't it stand to reason that my Heavenly Father also gave me a name that is meant to identify and distinguish me in His world? And don't I owe it to myself to discover what that name is?

Revelation 19:11-12 NLT

Then I saw heaven open. A white horse was standing there. The One Who was sitting on the horse is called Faithful and True. He is the One Who punishes in the right way. He makes war. [12]His eyes are a flame of fire. He has many crowns on His head. His name is written on Him but He is the only One Who knows what it says.

If the Lord Jesus has a name that no one knows but Himself, then I also believe that every human being has a name that no one knows except God. And that name is our eternal identity. Superman's parents called him Clark, but his biological parents called him Kal-El. Even though he discovered many of his powers before he knew his true identity, he didn't gain the confidence he needed to be Superman until he discovered who he truly was. It wasn't the power within him that gave him confidence it was the knowledge of his identity that gave him confidence. When we, as children of God, discover our spiritual identity, we will receive the confidence we need to live the extraordinary lives He created us to live.

My Own Words

Let me pause for a moment to say that I have had the privilege of preaching and teaching the things that I have written in this book numerous times, in many different places, on various occasions, for many years. Every word, phrase, and idea was born out of prayer and long days and nights of excavating truth from the word of God. Most of my days are spent writing or recording to try and keep up with all of the "God-thoughts" that are constantly flooding my heart and mind. The same is true for the words of this book. Even though the idea for this book was born out of that Superman movie, most of what I have written in this work came from sermons I constructed years before that fateful movie night in 2013.

The integrity of the creative process is very important to me, and unless otherwise stated, every word I pen to paper is my own. The reason I say this is because I have several pastor friends who have preached the insights I've shared with them with their congregations. None of these gentlemen did this behind my back or deceitfully. They are all sincere Men of God. They told me upfront that they would do it, and then they did. Though I don't mind this (as long as their source is referenced), it's important to me that every reader of this book knows that I am not taking words from anyone else's mouth to write this book or any of my projects, for that matter. I write my sermons and books the same way I write my poems. Prayerfully, carefully, laboriously and originally. To me, the process of creating the work is almost sweeter than the outcome.

There is perhaps no revelation that I have shared with some of my preacher friends that they have been more excited to deliver to their congregants than some of the contents of this work. There is also, nothing else I teach that I believe is more relevant and impactful to a follower of Christ than what I'm getting ready to share with you.

Identity Crisis

Hebrews 10:35 NKJV
Therefore, do not cast away your confidence, which has great reward.

Ephesians 1:18 NLT
I pray that your hearts will be flooded with light so that you can understand the confident hope he has given to those he called— his holy people who are his rich and glorious inheritance.

The church at Ephesus did not need God to give them anything more, they just needed to understand what God had already given them. What Paul was saying to them here was that the degree to which our hearts are filled with the light of God's truth is the same measure to which we will be confident in our expectation of accomplishing the things He wants us to do. Most of us are ineffective in our Christian lives, not because we don't have enough, but because we don't know enough about what we have. The Bible says that the early Church would pray that God would fill them with the power of the Holy Spirit. In addition to that, they also prayed for confidence.

Acts 4:29-30 VOICE

[29]And now, Lord, take note of their intimidations intended to silence us. Grant us, Your servants, the courageous confidence we need to go ahead and proclaim Your message [30]while You reach out Your hand to heal people, enabling us to perform signs and wonders through the name of Your holy servant Jesus.

That always puzzled me. I often wondered why they would need confidence if they already possessed the power of the Holy Spirit. It would seem as if having supernatural power would have made them confident. And that is true to some degree. The supernatural power of God gives you the confidence to do things you couldn't do if you didn't have that power. But no matter how much of the power of the Holy Spirit is flowing through you, it cannot be sustained in a person with a poor self-image and a dysfunctional mindset.

You can't cast out a dysfunctional mindset like it's a demon spirit. Nor can you get so full of the power of God that it overcomes your ignorance or your dysfunctional way of thinking. You have to re-train your mind by learning about your heavenly identity from the word of God. If you are weak in your knowledge of God's word, you will be weak in your ability to demonstrate the power of the Holy Spirit. That's why they prayed for power and for the boldness to demonstrate the power they possessed.

Crisis of Ignorance

One day, Jesus was approached by a religious sect called the Sadducees. They asked Him a theological hypothetical question about whether or not a woman who was a widow seven times over would be married to any of her seven husbands in eternity. Jesus told them that no one would be married to each other in eternity. We will be similar to the angels in this regard. But before He gave them this answer: He rebuked them for their foolish line of questioning.

Matthew 22:29 NLT

Jesus replied, "Your mistake is that you don't know the Scriptures, and you don't know the power of God. "

The Sadducees did not believe in the resurrection from the dead in the last days. And Jesus was making a connection between their inability to believe in the supernatural power of God and their misunderstanding of the Scriptures. So what Jesus was saying to them was the reason you don't believe in the greatest manifestation of the supernatural power of God (to snatch lives from the mouth of death) is that you don't understand the Scriptures. How many of us, like the Sadducees, are not experiencing the supernatural power of God in our lives, nor even believe in a global awakening in these last days because we just don't understand the Scriptures? If you are weak in your knowledge of God's Word, you will be weak in your ability to demonstrate the power of the Holy Spirit. It's a crisis of ignorance.

Joshua 1:8 VOICE

Let the words from the book of the law be always on your lips. Meditate on them day and night so that you may be careful to live by all that is written in them. If you do, as you make your way through this world, you will prosper and always find success.

Crisis of Revelation

I remember coming out of prayer meetings where my hands felt heavy and hot as if some sort of heat was emanating from them. Then the Holy Spirit would whisper in my heart. "Do you see that guy over there? Go and pray for him. I will use you to minister to him."

These types of things would happen on various occasions. And sometimes, I would disobey God. Not because I didn't believe He could do it but because I didn't believe He really wanted to use me to do these things. "I'm not a healing evangelist or a pastor. Why is God asking me to do these things? Maybe He's not. Maybe I'm imagining it." I would think to myself. I knew I was filled with the Holy Spirit and, therefore, possessed the power of God. I knew who God was to me, but I didn't really know who I was to Him, or who He was in me.

The great Warrior, Gideon of the Bible, also had an identity crisis. When we are first introduced to him in Judges Chapter 6, he's hiding. The reason he's hiding is because he has a legitimate reason to be afraid of Israel's enemies. For seven years, the Midianites had oppressed and terrorized his people. I've heard preachers make fun of Gideon for hiding from his enemies. He gets a bad rap for being afraid of the Midianites. But if you don't know God, and you don't know who you are as it relates to who He is, the smartest thing that you can be is afraid of the enemy that's seeking to devour you.

A guy once told me, "If I ever saw the Devil, I'd take a 12-gauge shotgun and blow his head off." The more we talked the more I realized he was not joking. Nor was he mentally challenged. I don't mean to sound harsh when I say this, but that guy was a fool. A fool is not someone who is just ignorant. What I mean is that a fool is not an ignorant person who doesn't know any better. A fool is someone who chooses ignorance over knowledge.

I wanted to explain to him that he couldn't literally harm the Devil With an earthly weapon, but he seemed like he might have that 12-

gauge shotgun nearby. So, I decided to let him win the argument. But the truth is, the real you, without God, is not a champion of faith. The real you without God is a coward. And if the real you without God is not a coward, then the real you without God is a fool. Because without Him, we should absolutely be afraid.

Judges 6:11-15 NLT

Then the angel of the LORD came and sat beneath the great tree at Ophrah, which belonged to Joash of the clan of Abiezer. Gideon son of Joash was threshing wheat at the bottom of a winepress to hide the grain from the Midianites. [12] The angel of the LORD appeared to him and said, "Mighty hero, the LORD is with you!" [13] "Sir," Gideon replied, "if the LORD is with us, why has all this happened to us? And where are all the miracles our ancestors told us about? Didn't they say, 'The LORD brought us up out of Egypt'? But now the LORD has abandoned us and handed us over to the Midianites." [14] Then the LORD turned to him and said, "Go with the strength you have, and rescue Israel from the Midianites. I am sending you!" [15] "But Lord," Gideon replied, "how can I rescue Israel? My clan is the weakest in the whole tribe of Manasseh, and I am the least in my entire family!"

What a poor self-image Gideon had. According to him, He was the least of the weakest. Rather than chastising Gideon for being afraid, God gives him a progressive revelation that builds his confidence in his ability to do the thing that God told him to do. God begins this progressive unveiling of truth by saying to Gideon, in verse 16, "I will be with you. And you will destroy the Midianites as if you were fighting against one man."

God assures Gideon of the two things that every person is afraid of, and overwhelmed by the obstacles in front of them needs to be assured of receiving faith. That is:

1. *"I will be with you"* = My Presence will be with you

2. *"You will destroy the Midianites as if you were fighting against one man."* = An extraordinary measure of My power will be in you.

He didn't just assure Gideon that He would defeat his enemy. He assured him that he would destroy his enemy as if his entire army was only fighting against one man. The greatest antidote to a lack of confidence is to be assured by God that His Presence is with you and His power is in you. The environment of His presence reveals what you need to know. And the operation of His power gives you the ability to do what you need to do. Notice that God did not just give Gideon his Presence and power. He first assured Gideon of His presence and power. Because the greatest antidote to the lack of confidence is not just Divine presence and power. It's the assurance that God's Presence is with you, and His power is in you. It's to hear from the one who created you assuring you that He is with you and in you to give you the victory.

Faith is not just when God gives you the ability to do the impossible. Faith is *knowing* that God has given you the ability to do the impossible. It's not just having the goods that makes the difference. It's knowing you have it.

The Clark Kent Crisis

The Clark Kent crisis is when you have worn the disguise of a normal, average, and ordinary existence for so long that you forget about your spiritual identity. Superman was not Clark Kent hoping to metamorphose into Superman. He was rather Superman, disguising himself and pretending to be Clark Kent. Though he grew up on Earth among earthlings, his real identity was not Clark Kent; it was Kal-El, the Kryptonian son of Jor-El. He was an extraordinary being, sent from an extraordinary place to an ordinary people to do extraordinary things.

In the classic 1980 movie, *Superman Part 2*, Superman, played by Christopher Reeves, no longer wanted to be Superman. He wanted to live an ordinary life like everyone else. He just wanted to live as Clark Kent, with Lois Lane, the love of his life. So, he gave up his superpowers in order to live the rest of his life as the ordinary man he was pretending to be. He wanted to fully live the life that, for so long, had camouflaged his extra-terrestrial identity.

James 1:22-25 NLV

"*...Anyone who hears the Word of God and does not obey is like a man looking at his face in a mirror. After he sees himself and goes away, he forgets what he looks like. But the one who keeps looking into God's perfect Law and does not forget it will do what it says and be happy as he does it...*"

James 1:22-25 MSG

"*...Those who hear and don't act are like those who glance in the mirror, walk away, and two minutes later have no idea who they are or what they look like. But whoever catches a glimpse of the revealed counsel of God—the free life!—even out of the corner of his eye and sticks with it is no distracted scatterbrain but a man or woman of action. That person will find delight and affirmation in the action.*"

The average Christian today thinks he is a natural man, hoping that with good works and occasional prayer, he will eventually metamorphose into a spiritual man. What he doesn't realize is that he is actually a spiritual man who is concealing his super natural identity under the disguise of an ordinary life.

He is not Clark Kent. He is Superman pretending to be Clark Kent. He's been pretending for so long now that he doesn't even realize he's traded in his spiritual identity for a counterfeit existence. Clark Kent is no longer a disguise to conceal who he really is. It's the illegitimate version of himself he has chosen to become.

Every time you read the word of God, you're looking in a mirror. The mirror's ultimate objective is not to show you your current image, falling short of the standard of Christ. Though you do see how short you fall of meeting that standard when you look in the mirror of God's word, that's not its ultimate objective. Its ultimate purpose is to reflect the image of Christ. Not just so that you can see Christ, but so that when you see Christ you realize that Christ was God's ultimate intention for man's design.

We gaze into the mirror of God's word, not just to see who Jesus is, but to see that who Jesus is everything that God originally created Adam to be. And the more we gaze into the mirror of His word the more we are changed into the image humanity was originally created to reflect!

Man's Origin

When we die, our bodies return to the Earth because that's where our bodies come from. But our spirits return to God because that's where our spirits come from. Our bodies come from Earth, and our spirits come from God.

Ecclesiastes 12:7 NLT

For then, the dust will return to the Earth, and the spirit will return to God who gave it.

When we understand where something is from, we are that much closer to understanding what it is for. We'll never understand what we came here for if we don't understand where we came here from. If you leave your country and get into trouble on foreign soil, if you're lucky, there are three questions the authorities will have for you. The first question is, "Who are you?" The second is "Where are you from?" The third is, "Why are you here?" These questions are all related to one another. Knowing who you are and where you are from gives them a better understanding of what they are dealing with. If they know who you are, but they don't know where you come from, then they won't be able to understand you in light of the people who know you best. Man's origin is God. So if we investigate God, we'll understand man. And we'll understand why God sent man into the Earth.

Romans 11:36 VOICE

For all that exists originates in Him, comes through Him, and is moving toward Him; so give Him the glory forever. Amen.

Man existed in God, was sent from God, and was empowered by God to live for God and then return to God. So man's odyssey through eternity and time, and back to eternity is in God, from God, by God, for God, and to God. Hallelujah!! To God be the glory!!

The reason for man being put on this planet is because God put His Kingdom in a man, then put that man in the Earth to bring everything above him, around him and underneath him under the government of Heaven.

Genesis 1:26-28 shows us that mankind was created in the image and likeness of God. Genesis 2:7 shows us that man was made of the dust of the ground and the breath of God. So because of that, mankind had the authority to be in the Earth because he was made of the Earth. He also had the authority to bring the Earth under the Kingdom of Heaven because he was made of and sent from Heaven. When we understand that mankind's origin is God, then we understand a little more about who he is and why he's here. As mankind, we have come from Heaven to Earth to bring Earth under the Kingdom of Heaven.

The Two YOUs

Jeremiah 1:5 NLT

"I knew you before I formed you in your mother's womb. Before you were born I set you apart and appointed you as my prophet to the nations."

Before God formed you (your body). He knew you (your spirit). If God knew you before He formed you, then you would have had to have existed before you were formed. Which means you had an eternal identity before you had an earthly existence. That's why He says, "Before I formed YOU, I knew YOU." He says "YOU," referring to who he formed. Your physical body. Then He says, YOU, referring to who He knew. Your eternal identity. Because the YOU He formed and the YOU He knew are two different YOU's. Let that thought sink in for a moment. I'm not suggesting that the physical part of you and the spiritual part of you are two different people. Absolutely not! I am, however, suggesting that you existed in the mind of God before you existed in the womb of your mother.

There is the YOU that God formed and the YOU that He knew. The You He formed, is the you that you know. But the You that existed before He formed you is the YOU that God knows. So, you relate to yourself according to what you know about "the YOU" you think you are. But God relates to you according to what He knows about who YOU really are.

Since God knew me before He formed me, then that means that I had an identity in Heaven before I had a body on the Earth. I had a heavenly identity before I had an earthly form. The real you is not the earthly shell that you bathe, dress, and feed every day. You don't have a body to just bathe it, feed it, and put it to sleep. You have a body because your eternal identity is an aspect of Heaven. And your body exists to give expression to the aspect of Heaven that lives within it. It exists to facilitate the needs of your spirit. Now that should make you want to run and shout! PLEASE take a coffee, tea, or bathroom break and meditate on that before you read any further. Because that was an earful.

Squeezed into Shape

The word "formed," used in Jeremiah 1:5, is the Hebrew word- 'yatzar.' It means to squeeze into shape. God knew your spirit before He formed your body. So when He got ready to form your body, He squeezed it into the shape of what He knew about your spirit. He squeezed your earthly existence into the shape of your eternal identity. It doesn't mean that your body looks like or is in the shape of your spirit. It means that your body is specifically designed to house no other human spirit than yours. God carefully and specifically crafted your human body to house your eternal identity. The two are perfectly comparable and compatible.

The God who carefully crafted and molded the masculinity of the first man from the Earth, and framed the femininity of the first woman from the man; has put as much love, care, and detail in forming, in the womb, every man and every woman that has ever existed. He didn't just get the ball of human existence rolling with Adam, and then take His hands off of the rest of us. He has personally created, touched, handled, and watched over every embryo, fetus, and beating heart. Throughout the entire nine months you were in your mother's womb; God was forming you, and watching over you in the most vulnerable stages of your development.

You vs. You

Jeremiah 1:6 NLT

"'O Sovereign LORD,' I said, 'I can't speak for you! I'm too young!'"

God tells Jeremiah that he's a prophet, and Jeremiah doesn't respond to God according to God's knowledge of him. He responds to God according to his own knowledge of himself. He pretty much tells God, "I appreciate the offer, but I have to turn it down because I'm not qualified. How crazy is that? But it should not come as a surprise to us that he did that because many of us do the same thing all the time. The devil is not the greatest enemy of your destiny; you are. More specifically, disobedience, insecurity, and unbelief are the greatest enemies of your destiny. The reason I know the devil is not the greatest enemy of my destiny is because he doesn't have the ability to destroy it like I do. The devil's hatred of me is not nearly as dangerous to me as my stubbornness to God.

Jeremiah 1:7 NLT

The LORD replied, "Don't say, 'I'm too young,' for you must go wherever I send you and say whatever I tell you.

God

"Stop talking to me about the YOU that I formed when I just finished telling you about the you that existed before I formed you. The YOU that you know is an insecure, terrified child, but the YOU that I know is a mighty courageous Prophet!"

When God is telling you about His plans for your life, He's not speaking of what you've come to know about yourself throughout the years. He's speaking of the glorious things He has always known about you. And He's trying to get you to see yourself through His eyes.

Jeremiah 1:8 NLT

⁸And don't be afraid of the people, for I will be with you and will protect you. I, the LORD, have spoken!"

The King James Version says, "Don't be afraid of their faces." The reason why we are afraid of people is because we are more aware of people than we are of God. If we were more aware of God's face, then we couldn't be afraid of the faces of the people He has sent us to. People who already have the approval of God are not afraid of the disapproval of men. Wow!! Say that over and over again until you accept it, believe it, and receive it.

The Greatest Hindrance to the Supernatural

The greatest hindrances to the supernatural power of God operating in the life of the believer is the lack of faith.

Hebrews 11:6 TLB

You can never please God without faith, without depending on him. Anyone who wants to come to God must believe that there is a God and that he rewards those who sincerely look for him.

What most of us call faith is just wishful thinking disguised in faith's clothes. But that's not real faith. Real faith is the confidence you get from having spiritual evidence for something you cannot yet physically see. The greatest hindrance to the supernatural today is a lack of real faith. But it goes deeper than that. There is not just one level of faith. There are three levels of faith.

1. When God becomes God to you. It's when you realize that your God and Creator is your Redeemer, Lord, Father, Friend, Counselor, Advocate, Protector, and King.

Psalm 118:28 NLT
You are my God, and I will praise you! You are my God, and I will exalt you!

Psalm 63:1 NLT
O God, you are my God ...

2. The next level of faith is when God becomes God in you. It's when you realize that your Creator and King live inside you.

Colossians 1:27 NKJV
To them God willed to make known what are the riches of the glory of this

mystery among the Gentiles: which is Christ in you, the hope of glory.

1 Corinthians 3:16 NLT
Do you not know that you are a house of God and that the Holy Spirit lives in you?

3. When God becomes God through you. It's when you release what God has put in you to affect the world around you.

Matthew 5:16 NLT

Let your light shine in front of men. Then they will see the good things you do and will honor your Father Who is in heaven.

2 Corinthians 2:14 VOICE

Yet I am so thankful to God, who always marches us to victory under the banner of the Anointed One; and through us He spreads the beautiful fragrance of His knowledge to every corner of the earth.

Most of us realize that God is God to us. What we don't realize is that He's also God in us. And because we don't realize that, He rarely becomes God through us to affect the world around us. You can't have faith in God beyond the things that you have allowed God to reveal to you about Himself.

If you've been a Christian for any number of years, you understand this point. What you still may not understand, however, is something that many Christians aren't aware of. That is, you can't have faith in your ability to be used by God beyond those things that you have allowed God to reveal to you about yourself. Now, we're going into deeper waters.

It's the God in Me

You may remember the 2008 gospel hit song by the singing group Mary Mary, "God in Me." Those three words are more profound than many of us realize. The Holy Spirit within us is just as much God in us as He is God to us.

Most of us, as Christians, don't struggle with the concept of God's ability to be God. Most of us struggle with the concept of God's ability to be as much God in our hearts as He is in His Heaven. It is as if God is a gigantic God in His Heaven and a miniature God in our hearts. We believe that God is big on His throne, but somewhere along the line, we adopted the lie that His nature is somehow diminished when it takes up residency within us.

Our problem is not that we don't believe that He is who He said He is. Our problem is that we don't believe that we are who He said we were. We somehow believe that the Holy Spirit that resides in us is a diluted and diminished version of the Holy Spirit that resided in Paul, Peter, James, and John. But the Bible says in Romans 8:11, *"The Spirit of God, who raised Jesus from the dead, lives in you. And just as God raised Christ Jesus from the dead, He will give life to your mortal bodies by this same Spirit living within you."* God is not big on His throne and small when He takes up occupancy in you! God is always the same size!

There are measures and degrees of His presence and power that He gives to us as we need it or are able to contain it. But you don't have a smaller version of God than someone you consider to be more powerful than yourself. There is no such thing as a pulpit-size God for the preacher and a pew-size God for the church member. God is the one who hung the stars, molded the mountains, carved out the valleys, stretched out the heavens, and uses the Earth as His footstool. This is God. And it is this same God that dwells in the hearts of His followers. It's not some watered-down version of Him. So, if God is in you, then it is GOD that is in you!! He diminishes none of His attributes to relate to you or take up occupancy within you. Instead, He makes you more and more like Himself.

Watch Your Mouth

⁹Then the LORD reached out and touched my mouth and said, "Look, I have put my words in your mouth! ¹⁰Today I appoint you to stand up against nations and kingdoms. Some you must uproot and tear down, destroy and overthrow. Others you must build up and plant."

God touches Jeremiah's mouth to stop him from talking. Jeremiah didn't realize that he was talking himself out of what God was trying to talk him into. In essence, God was telling him, "Stop saying what you think about yourself because you are so much more than what you think! So until you change the way you think, stop talking!" Oh, that we could feel the fingertips of the Heavenly Father on our lips of clay, sternly warning us about our words.

Yes, how we desperately need the holy rebuke of our Heavenly King, helping us to bite our tongue and listen before we speak.

Matthew 12:36-37 NLT

[36] "And I tell you this, you must give an account on judgment day for every idle word you speak. [37] The words you say will either acquit you or condemn you."

How sobering. No one in their right mind would go about their day throwing the cash in their pockets on the ground everywhere they went. That's crazy! No one would be that careless with their money. Yet so many of us are just that careless with our words.

We say anything and everything that comes to our minds. We speak of ourselves in the most demeaning of terms. I often wonder, when I hear people say things like, "I'm stupid," or "I'm never going to be anything in life," if they really know what they're saying. I get angry about things like this. I want to pull them aside and say, "Don't you know that you have no right to talk about yourself this way!?"

What angers me so much about this is that I used to speak of myself in similar terms. I thought I wasn't valuable because of a learning disability that I had as a child. I was in special education, from the third through the eighth grade. I rode the short bus to school. I stood in a doctor's office in Baltimore, MD. The doctor informed my mother that I had a neurological dysfunction that would prohibit me from ever being able to articulate myself properly. When she informed him that she and my father believed I was called by God to preach the gospel, he laughed her to scorn and said, "Don't fill this boy's head with false hopes. He will never be able to articulate himself as other people are able to, especially not before a crowd of people."

My mother wishes she could remember that doctor's name, and send him some of my recorded sermons today. But long before I came to God and began to understand who I was as it relates to Him, I had severe low self-esteem.

It stemmed from teachers who called me words like dumb, stupid, idiot, slow, and worthless. Only a few of them said things like that to me. But it was enough to do damage. Most of them just looked at me, like they were sorry for me. The truth is that felt even worse than calling me stupid. Because it made me feel like they were right to feel sorry for me. It made me feel sorry for myself. Sorry that I was even born. Those teachers that weren't mean to me or sorry for me, just seemed annoyed that they had to teach a student that was as slow as I was.

"Maybe I am to be pitied." I thought. "Maybe I should kill myself." The seeds of rejection, depression, and suicide were sown into my heart. I started cursing, drinking alcohol, smoking cigarettes and marijuana, and hanging with the wrong crowd. The insightful and inspirational poetry that I once wrote was now dark and hopeless. My words were a reflection of what I thought I was worth.

But when I had an encounter with the presence and power of Jesus Christ, at age 15, it transformed my life. When I met Him, I met me. I realized, "So you were the one who created me! You are nothing like I thought you were, and I'm nothing like I thought I was." The devil lied to me about my identity because he knew that if I ever discovered who I really was, I would realize my true value and start agreeing with God instead of agreeing with him. And the devil has no power over a person whose words and ways come into agreement with God.

The next time that you are inclined to speak negatively about yourself, remember this. You didn't create yourself, so you have no right to determine your own value. God created you, and He has already determined your value. When Jesus died on the cross, that was God demonstrating to the world how much every human being is worth to Him. The reason that God became a man and gave His own life in exchange for yours is because that is what He considers your life to be worth. The currency of God's life is what it costs God to acquire the merchandise of your soul. Now that makes me want to shout!

The Prophet or the Child

Jeremiah 1:11-12 NLT

[11] Then the LORD said to me, "Look, Jeremiah! What do you see?" And I replied, "I see a branch from an almond tree." [12] And the LORD said, "That's right, and it means that I am watching, and I will certainly carry out all my plans." [13] Then the LORD spoke to me again and asked, "What do you see now?"

And I replied, "I see a pot of boiling water, spilling from the north." Why did God ask Jeremiah this question? The first time I read it, it seemed strange to me. Jeremiah is struggling with his self-image, and God seems to jump ahead a few steps and ask him what he sees. "God, what does it matter? He's not embraced his prophetic ministry, so he probably sees nothing." That is what I was thinking when I first read this text. But I was wrong. Here's what's really going on in this passage of Scripture as I see it.

Jeremiah sees himself as a child, and God sees him as a Prophet. Throughout this entire conversation, God speaks to the child about being a prophet. But in verse 11, God stops speaking to the child and starts speaking to the Prophet. God stopped speaking to who Jeremiah knew himself as and started addressing who He knew Jeremiah to be.

When God stopped speaking to the child about the Prophet, and started speaking directly to Jeremiah's Prophetic identity, the child shut up, and the Prophet within him started speaking up. Before God can really use you for His glory; you've got to be determined to stop being the child and start being the Prophet. You have to see yourself as He sees you.

The reason that God asked Jeremiah what he saw is because He just told him that he was a Prophet. At the most basic level, a Prophet's responsibility is to see in the realm of the spirit and then say what he sees. So God, in essence, was actually making a point to Jeremiah. "If you don't believe that you're really a Prophet, then why is it that you have the ability to see prophetically? You can argue with me, but let's see how well you argue with the things I'm about to reveal to you." Wow! That is incredible. God momentarily ignores Jeremiah's intellect and emotions and speaks directly to the prophetic gift within him.

Here is the order of events that led to Jeremiah's prophetic ministry:

1. God tells Jeremiah that he's a Prophet.
2. Jeremiah objects to being a Prophet.
3. God ignores Jeremiah's objections and starts placing a demand on the prophetic gift that Jeremiah doesn't even believe he's qualified to possess.

What I have come to realize in my 47 years on this Earth is that God doesn't need your permission to go after His own investment! If He made a deposit in your life, then even without your permission He's going to place a demand on the thing He deposited within you.

Ask Jonah about this. He'll say God gives us all a will, but I don't know how free that will is. It costs a whole lot to choose your will over His. As I often say from the pulpit, free will ain't free; it's expensive.

Isaiah 55:10-11 NLT

¹⁰"The rain and snow come down from the heavens and stay on the ground to water the earth. They cause the grain to grow, producing seed for the farmer and bread for the hungry. ¹¹It is the same with my word. I send it out, and it always produces fruit. It will accomplish all I want it to, and it will prosper everywhere I send it.

If God sends you His word, and you decide that you don't want to follow it to the place of its fulfillment, the word he gave you will be accomplished with or without you. Jeremiah struggled with God's word about his identity and destiny. But if he ultimately rejected God's word, then God would have raised up someone else to become a Prophet to the nations. His prophetic identity would not have been taken from him, but his prophetic assignment would have been hindered. God would have had to appoint someone else to stand up against nations and Kingdoms, uproot, tear down, destroy, overthrow, build, and plant because that was the purpose of the word. It wasn't just the calling of Jeremiah, it was to call Jeremiah to accomplish this purpose. Because the Word of God is not obligated to the person or people to whom it is spoken. It is only obligated to accomplish the purpose of which it speaks. God's Word does not belong to any individual. It belongs to the assignment that the individual has been given. As long as you are obedient to accomplish the assignment God gives you, His Word can be accomplished in your life. It includes you and involves you but it's not about you. It's about what God has purposed and planned for His glory and our good.

The Real You

> [11] *"I see a branch from an almond tree..."* [14] *"I see a pot of boiling water, spilling from the north..."*

In the midst of his fear and insecurities, Jeremiah sees things in the spirit realm that he has never seen before. His eternal identity is speaking up. The prophetic gift within him started functioning without his permission. I have been preaching since I was 16 years old. I preached my first sermon under a tent in my homeland, Jamaica, where I was born. When I was 20 years old, for about a six-month period, I was consumed with the desire to preach the gospel everywhere and all the time. It was all I could think about. It wasn't unusual for me to want to preach. But this seemed almost obsessive. It was as if something within me was driving me to look for places to preach and people to preach to. I prayed and asked the Lord what was wrong with me. He assured me that nothing was wrong with me. He spoke to me, not audibly, but inwardly, and said, "It's not you that wants to preach. It's the gift within you that's seeking to find the place it was destined for." All I could imagine was that I was like Bill Bixby's character, David Banner, in the 1978 classic TV series, *The Incredible Hulk*, and the gift of preaching within me was the incredible Hulk trying to break forth and run free.

Without Jeremiah's permission, the gift within him was doing the same thing. It was breaking forth and running free! These prophecies of his are the first he's ever uttered. They are not the bold declarations of a mighty prophet. They are rather the divine revelations of a startled child who has just been introduced to His prophetic identity. This is the first time that Jeremiah has ever prophesied in His life. And just 15 seconds ago, he couldn't fathom the notion that he could ever be a Prophet. Wow!!! Think about that. A few moments ago, he is objecting to the idea of being a prophet, and just a few moments later, he is passionately making prophetic declarations.

So, he is not prophesying now because he has suddenly reconciled himself to the idea of becoming a Prophet. He is not declaring these messages from God with the tone of a seasoned orator. If you read this passage and imagine Jeremiah speaking with the homiletical ability of Dr. Martin Luther King, Jr. or Charles Spurgeon while standing with a professorial poise, you're reading it wrong. He wasn't prophesying with great assurance. I believe he was prophesying in great amazement that these words were even coming out of his mouth! And that's what happens when you meet the real you! You're amazed by the rush of conviction and confidence that floods your awareness when your eternal identity is ignited and your inner man is awakened!

Who Is He? Who Are You?

When God introduces you to the real you, it blows your mind. Because it's not something that you could ever be without Him. It starts with a revelation of God and then leads to a revelation of self. That's what happened to Peter in Matthew Chapter 16.

Matthew 16:13-21 NLT

¹³When Jesus came to the region of Caesarea Philippi, he asked his disciples, "Who do people say that the Son of Man is?" ¹⁴"Well," they replied, "some say John the Baptist, some say Elijah, and others say Jeremiah or one of the other prophets."" ¹⁵Then he asked them, "But who do you say I am?" ¹⁶Simon Peter answered, "You are the Messiah, the Son of the living God." ¹⁷Jesus replied, "You are blessed, Simon son of John, because my Father in heaven has revealed this to you. You did not learn this from any human being. ¹⁸ Now I say to you that you are Peter (which means 'rock'), and upon this rock I will build my church, and all the powers of hell will not conquer it. ¹⁹ And I will give you the keys of the Kingdom of Heaven. Whatever you forbid on earth will be forbidden in heaven, and whatever you permit on earth will be permitted in heaven." ²⁰Then he sternly warned the disciples not to tell anyone that he was the Messiah. ²¹From then on Jesus began to tell his disciples plainly that it was necessary for him to go to Jerusalem, and that he would suffer many terrible things at the hands of the elders, the leading priests, and the teachers of religious law. He would be killed, but on the third day he would be raised from the dead.

In this passage, Peter gets a revelation of Jesus' Messianic identity. Then Jesus gives Peter the revelation of his spiritual identity. Roman Catholicism confused this passage to mean that Jesus was building His Church on the Apostle Peter. But that's incomplete and not at all the point of what was happening here. Here's the whole story as I see it. Peter got a revelation of who Jesus was, and Jesus gave Peter a revelation of who Peter was.

Jesus is about to take His disciples to the next level in their relationship with Him. But some things have to be revealed to them before He can take them there. These revelations are about who Jesus really is, and who they really are as it relates to Him. He is building His Church on the revelation of Himself as the Lord of the Church. But He's not building it on that alone. Christ is the Chief cornerstone, but there are other stones that have to be put in place.

Here's what I believe is the meaning of what the Lord was saying and doing in this exchange between He and Peter. He was demonstrating how He builds His Church. God's revelation of Himself doesn't build the Church, because He has always known who He is. He builds it on our revelation of who He is! His Church gets built when you see Him, and start declaring what you see! Jesus first started talking about the Church when Peter saw Him for who he really was and started saying what he saw.

It's no coincidence that this is the first time that the word Church, (Ecclesia in the Greek text), is mentioned in the Bible. There is a reason it's introduced to us in this context. I think it's possible that it is mentioned first in this context because Peter saw Jesus' true identity, and the concept of the Church is exactly this. It's not a place where people go every Sunday. It's God having a relationship with a people who know Him for who He really is. The same way that Adam knew God in the Garden. The Church is the restoration of mankind having that kind of relationship with God again.

Relationship starts at the place of revelation. Adam saw God for who

God was, and God could be Himself with Adam. A husband and wife can't have a real relationship with each other without intellectually and emotionally revealing themselves to one another. In the same way, our relationship with God only begins when He reveals Himself to us and also reveals to us the aspects of ourselves we never knew!

Peter didn't just say, "You're the Messiah!" and they all cheered happily and went home. No. Jesus responded to Peter's declaration by telling Peter who he was as well. Jesus did not need Peter to identify Him. But Peter needed to identify Jesus, so that Jesus could, in turn, identify Peter.

The principle we understand from this is that hidden within your revelation of God's identity is the revelation of your identity! Wow! Stop for a few minutes and ponder that. Hidden within the revelation of who God really is, is the revelation of who you really are.

If you've discovered who you are without discovering who Jesus is, then you have discovered an illegitimate version of yourself. Or you have discovered a legitimate version of yourself illegitimately.

Ephesians 2:20-22 NLT

²⁰ Together, we are his house, built on the foundation of the apostles and the prophets. And the cornerstone is Christ Jesus himself. ²¹ We are carefully joined together in him, becoming a holy temple for the Lord. ²² Through him you Gentiles are also being made part of this dwelling where God lives by his Spirit.

God is building His Church on the foundation of the revelation of who He is as it relates to us and who we are as it relates to Him. Glory be to God! That is awesome!

Seven major things took place here in Caesarea Philippi:

1. Peter got a revelation of who Jesus was.

2. Peter got a revelation of who Peter was.

3. A new kind of intimacy began between the two parties whose spiritual identities were just revealed.

4. Out of this intimacy came a brand-new relationship between

Jesus and His disciples that gave birth to the Church.

5. Jesus prophetically declared the level of dominion that His Church would have over the powers of the Kingdom of Darkness.

6. Divine authority was given after eternal identification took place.

7. Jesus gave his disciples insight concerning things to come that He never talked to them about before. Because God only reveals what He plans to do to those who have received a revelation of who He is.

How do all of these seven things apply to you?

1. When you get a revelation of who Jesus is...

2. He will show you who you really are.

3. When He does, you'll experience an intimacy with Him that you have never known.

4. Out of that intimacy, you'll birth sons and daughters into the Kingdom (win souls to Christ and disciple them).

5. You'll then be able to take dominion over the powers of darkness. (you'll walk in power and authority over demonic strongholds and hindrances).

6. You will receive authorization from God to enter new corridors of His Kingdom.

7. And then God will be able to disclose some things to you that you have never known before.

Let's look at this passage in the Message Bible.

Matthew 16:13-19

The Message

13 When Jesus arrived in the villages of Caesarea Philippi, he asked his disciples, "What are people saying about who the Son of Man is?" 14 They replied, "Some think he is John the Baptizer, some say Elijah, some Jeremiah or one of the other prophets." ¹⁵He pressed them, "And how about you? Who do you say I am?" ¹⁶Simon Peter said, "You're the Christ, the Messiah, the Son of the living God." ¹⁷⁻¹⁸Jesus came back, "God bless you, Simon, son of Jonah! You didn't get that answer out of books or from teachers. My Father in heaven, God himself, let you in on this secret of who I really am. And now I'm going to tell you who you really are. You are Peter, a rock. This is the rock on which I will put together my church, a church so expansive with energy that not even the gates of hell will be able to keep it out. ¹⁹"And that's not all. You will have complete and free access to God's kingdom, keys to open any and every door: no more barriers between heaven and earth, earth and heaven. A yes on earth is yes in heaven. A no on earth is no in heaven."

Now, here's my breakdown and explanation of this passage.

"You are blessed, Simon, son of Jonah. Because your earthly father, Jonah, didn't reveal this secret to you, my heavenly father Jehovah revealed it to you. So now I get to reveal to you who you really are. Because the revelation of who you really are is hidden in your revelation of who I really am.

You are a precious and powerful rock. A very significant part of a spiritual residence I'm building to establish my Kingdom, and house my presence in the Earth. There are more stones to come, but your revelation of the Chief cornerstone has set you in your rightful place next to me, and accelerated this construction process.

This spiritual house, made up of living stones, will also be an army of warriors, so powerful the Kingdom of darkness will not be able to keep them from advancing into territories it is trying to hold hostage.

Since my Heavenly Father revealed this secret to you about the identity of THE Son of God, then you must be a Son of God. Because my Father doesn't reveal His secrets to strangers, He only reveals them to His sons. For the secrets of the Lord are only shared with those who fear Him.

And since you are a son of the King, I therefore authorize you to receive the keys to your Father's house. The gates and doors of the Kingdom of

God. You will have complete and free access to God's Kingdom; keys to open doors to heavenly dimensions. No more barriers between Heaven and Earth. The resources of Heaven will be completely at your disposal to fully supply you with whatever you need to help you bring Earth under Heaven's government.

CHAPTER 10
THY KINGDOM COME

The title of this book sums up my objective in writing it. That objective is to bring the reader to the understanding that God's original intention for creating us was to make us His Aliens. He wants all His children to understand their spiritual identity in His Kingdom as Anointed lives invading the world supernaturally. He also wants us to know that there is nothing spooky or strange about someone who is anointed by His Spirit and impacting their sphere of the world with His supernatural power. It is my prayer that all of this has been sufficiently communicated in every word you have read thus far.

However, as important as it is for us to gain a biblical perspective of our roles in God's Kingdom, there is nothing more important than understanding that it's all about the King. We must never forget that. No Kingdom is more important than its King. And the Kingdom of God is a reflection of the eternal magnificence of His holy majesty, King Jesus. All of the talk about the Kingdom of God nowadays is great and much needed. But we must remember that if it doesn't revolve around the King of the Kingdom, it's all irrelevant. Including this book. The prayer, "Your Kingdom Come. Your will be done on Earth as it is in Heaven" was more than a prayer. It was Jesus teaching His disciples to develop a lifelong pursuit. That pursuit would not make them experts in the Kingdom of God, but rather portals for the Kingdom of God to enter into the world. It would also cause them to live the kind of lives that attracted the Presence of their Holy King.

As a skinny 15-year-old boy in Randallstown, Maryland, the words of that prayer captured my heart and constantly rolled off my tongue. It flooded my days and filled my nights with billowing waves of heavenly joy and ferocious flames of holy love. It didn't create a desire in me to debate about a pre-, mid-, or post-tribulation rapture. It rather created a desire to pray until I felt as if I had been raptured. I wasn't longing for some distant political government to prove my eschatological perspective through a plethora of apocalyptic events. I was longing for the all-consuming presence of the One who visited me at 15 years old in my bedroom to reveal Himself to everyone I knew, the way He revealed Himself to me.

If your pastor's teaching on the Kingdom of God causes you to be more afraid of end-time terrorists than hungry for an end-time outpouring of God's Presence, then He's not teaching about the Kingdom. He's using the subject of the Kingdom to impose his carnal perspective of spiritual things on you. Because true Kingdom teaching doesn't create panic; it creates a biblical perspective of the Kingdom and a holy passion for the Presence of the King!

Building for His Presence

The Churches, lives, and careers that we are building must ultimately be for the Glory of King Jesus. What we must ask ourselves in the Church today is not so much "What are we building?" but rather, "What are we building for?" If you're building a marriage, a family, a business, or a Church, why are you building it? What do you want the outcome to be? Are you building a marriage, because you are lonely? Are you building a family because your Parents want grandchildren? Are you building a career to keep up with the Jones'? Are you building a Church because you can make a decent living, hobnob with political officials, and be respected by your community? What are you building for? Why are you working on your master's degree? Why are you becoming a mentor? All of these things, in and of themselves, are great. But why are you doing it? What's your motive?

In Exodus 25:8, God gave the best reason why His people should build anything, when He said to Moses:

"Let them build a sanctuary for me so that I can dwell among them."

The entire purpose of building something for the Kingdom of God

A.L.I.E.N.S.

is so that whatever you're building becomes a place that is able to house the Presence of God! The purpose of your marriage is not for you to be happy. The purpose of your career is not for you to be successful. The purpose of your family is not so that you can have something to talk about with your co-workers who also have families. The purpose of your marriage, family, home, career, and Church is to become a Sanctuary for the presence of God to dwell in. That's right! The Church building is not the only place that should contain a sanctuary for God's Presence. Every part of your life should be a sanctuary for God's presence to dwell.

Is God's presence everywhere or somewhere?

God is omnipresent. That means that His presence is everywhere. So why is the God who is already everywhere telling Moses that He desires to be somewhere? If He's everywhere all the time, then why's He telling Moses that He desires to be somewhere at a point in time?

How is it that throughout the Scriptures, the God, who is always where everybody is, constantly agonizes over His desire to be where a certain people are? The one whose presence is everywhere does not show up just anywhere and longs to manifest His presence somewhere. This is a theological paradox. It's a seeming contradiction.

Psalm 100:2 KJV

Serve the Lord with gladness: come before his presence with singing.

Psalm 95:2 ESV

Let us come into his presence with thanksgiving;

If God is omnipresent, then why does He tell us to come into His Presence? Or why do we have to invite His Presence and Kingdom into our lives? Why pray, "Your Kingdom come..." if all things already exist in Him? This confused me for many years. I've heard great teachings on the Presence of God, but I never really understood the reason why I had to invite God's Presence into my life if everyone and everything is already in God's Presence.

I finally understood this when I sat down and thought it through. Some things God reveals to you by His Spirit. Other things He allows you to use your brain to connect the dots. It would do many of us some good from time to time, to sit down in silence and think about the Scriptures. The Bible calls it meditating on the word. After pondering these things for a while, I finally understood it.

Though God's Presence is everywhere, He doesn't manifest His Presence just anywhere. That's why He told Moses, "Let them build a sanctuary for me so that I can dwell, live, and abide with them." Because though everyone on the planet is experiencing the omnipresence of God, only those who have prepared a place for Him to dwell are experiencing the manifested Presence of God. WOW! Consider that for a moment. The manifested Presence of God is the Spirit of God manifested into your physical world. It's the visible evidence that God's invisible Spirit has invaded the physical world.

I've heard preachers and worship leaders pray from the pulpit, "Lord, I'm not going to pray for your Presence to come because you're everywhere. And you were already here when we got here. So just make us more aware of your presence." And though I understand where they're coming from, that's not entirely true. I believe and preach about the need for God's people to be more aware of the dimensions and benefits of the Presence of God.

But there is a difference between the omnipresence of God and the manifested presence of God. The omnipresence of God is already everywhere, all the time, but God's manifested presence is not. It's only in certain places, at certain times. The evidence of the omnipresence of God is your ability to inhale and exhale. The evidence of the manifested Presence of God is your inability to remain standing when the glory of God floods the room. Whether or not you experience the manifested Presence of God is not up to God, it's up to you. It depends entirely on whether or not you invite His Kingdom to come and invade your world.

Attracting the Kingdom

When Jesus told us to pray, "Thy Kingdom Come..." He doesn't just want our lips to ask for the Kingdom. He wants our lives to attract it. In the Church today, many of us are asking for the manifested Presence of God, but our Lives are not attracting His manifested presence. So, how do we attract the King and His Kingdom?

Exodus 25:10-11, 20-22 NLT

[10] "Have the people make an Ark of acacia wood—a sacred chest 45 inches long, 27 inches wide, and 27 inches high. [11] Overlay it inside and outside with pure gold, and run a molding of gold all around it...

[20] The cherubim will face each other and look down on the atonement cover. With their wings spread above it, they will protect it. [21] Place inside the Ark the stone tablets inscribed with the terms of the covenant, which I will give to you. Then put the atonement cover on top of the Ark. [22] I will meet with you there and talk to you from above the atonement cover between the gold cherubim that hover over the Ark of the Covenant. From there, I will give you my commands for the people of Israel.

The Ark of the Covenant was the only piece of furniture in the Tabernacle that directly attracted the presence and glory of God! And when God told Moses to build the Tabernacle, He told him to build the Ark of the Covenant first, and then build everything else around it! What God was trying to communicate is that the first thing that we need to build in His house, and as His house is the thing that attracts the presence of God, and then we need to build everything else around the thing that attracts His presence. So, before we get too caught up in building anything, we must first develop a life that attracts the Presence of God, and then build and arrange everything else in our lives around that.

If the first thing the early Church built were lives that attracted the Presence of God, then the first things that we should build are lives that attract God's Presence. We should spend time building a prayer life, and deepening our study of the word of God. And just like the lives of the six-winged Seraphim in Isaiah Six revolve around the throne, even so our lives must also revolve around God's throne. And the more our life revolves around the throne, the more the Holy Spirit will reveal to us about the One that sits upon it.

The reason the Apostles were so powerful is because every one of them lived a consecrated life that attracted the Presence of God. And they built everything else in their life around it. They lived a consecrated life, and then they built their programs and projects around their consecrated lifestyle. We do the opposite in the Church today. We build what we're attracted to and hope that God shows up and blesses us anyway.

The Missing Ark

From the time of King Josiah, and the Prophet Jeremiah to the time of John the Baptist, the Ark of the Covenant was missing from the Temple, and no one knows exactly where it went. Isn't it interesting that the only piece of furniture in the Tabernacle from which God told Moses He would manifest His Presence, was the only piece of furniture that ended up missing. The Priests of John the Baptist's day were content to continue their daily religious ministries and duties in the Temple, even though the only thing that was designed to attract the Presence of God to the Temple was missing!

Every other piece of furniture served the purpose of ministering to the needs of men so that men could get into the Presence of God. The Ark was the only piece of furniture that was made exclusively for God! This is a picture of much of the Church today. Many leaders in the Church are content to go on with their everyday ritualistic routines in the house of God when the very lifestyle of obedience, prayer, and true worship, which are the only things guaranteed to attract God's Presence is missing!! John's father was Zechariah, a priest. According to Hebrew tradition it was customary for the son of a priest to follow in the footsteps of his father and also become a priest. If John became a priest like his father, then he too would have had to serve in a temple where the Ark was missing! But God defied tradition and called John to be a prophet!

The prophetic mantle on his life caused him not to be content to minister in a religious facade that no longer had the capacity to attract the presence of God! I believe there's a generation in the Earth today, like John the Baptist, that is disgusted with the thought of continuing a religious facade called the Church that no longer possesses the only components that have the capacity to attract the Presence of God! The Temple was elaborate and extraordinary, but it no longer attracted God's presence. And though much of what we're doing in the Church today is

A.L.I.E.N.S.

elaborate and extraordinary; much of what we're doing is not attracting the presence of God! This generation is not desperate to sit in a pew or stand in a pulpit, they're desperate to experience the presence and power of God.

Our Churches have the lights, the cameras, and the ascetics down pat. We even have great music and great preaching and teaching. What's missing is the one thing that attracts the manifested presence of God. And that's people who will arrange and rearrange everything in their lives around their determination to attract God's presence.

When David became King, His first order of business was not about politics; it was about the presence of God. He wanted to bring the Ark of the Covenant back to where it belonged. The thing I love about David is that he wasn't too proud to admit that the presence of God was missing. King Saul never even inquired about the Ark of the Covenant, but David refused to govern the Kingdom without it. He refused to be King without God's presence. As the old folks used to say, "I know in my knower," that God is raising up Davidic Worshipers! These are people who are not too proud to admit that God's Presence is missing from God's house. If we want the presence of God to return to the people of God, we've got to be honest enough to admit that it's missing. It blows my mind that the priests of John's day were content to minister in a place where the very piece of furniture that hosted God's presence was missing. So they were ministering every day in a place where God wasn't being ministered to. Wow! What a tragedy! To minister to everyone else's needs except God's needs.

Every day, some sort of ministry was taking place in the Temple. At the Brazen Alter, the sacrifices would be slaughtered. But there was no Ark to sprinkle the blood upon. Redemption is not complete until the blood of Jesus enters the presence of God. At the Brazen Laver, the priests were cleansing themselves. But there was no anointing to walk in purity. At the Menorah, they would keep the lamps burning. But there was no power to keep the fire burning in their hearts.

At the Table of Showbread, they were either eating the bread on the Sabbath day, or watching over it during the week. The Table of Showbread was also known as the "Bread of His Presence" because it was supposed to sit in the presence of God for a whole week before it was eaten. But though there was no Ark in the Temple, they were still baking and eating the bread. How many of us have gone to Churches where there is no presence of God, but the preacher is still preaching the word of God? And because of the quality of the word, we ignore the fact that God's presence isn't present.

At the Golden Altar, the fragrance of incense was kept burning continually. But the fragrance of His presence was no longer there. There was a lot of ministry going on in the Temple, all the time, but there was no Ark. It's possible for ministry to take place on a daily basis without the presence of God. Leonard Ravenhill said, "You can have all of your doctrines right—yet still not have the presence of God."

Most people decide what Church they're going to go to based on the power of the word the preacher preaches! God decides what Church He's going to go to based on the purity of the worship the people give Him! Most people chose their Churches based on the degree to which they feel that it minister to them. God chooses the Church He goes to based on the degree to which He feels it ministers to Him! Because God understands that when you minister to Him, He, in turn, ministers to you.

At the time of this writing, the total time I've pastored altogether is 14 years. There was a season during those 14 years when I was consumed with the desire to start new projects to minister to the community. I was coming up with all sorts of ideas and projects to start. I was so consumed by it that I became really stressed. I was losing lots of sleep worried about how I would minister to my community. The Lord spoke to me during this time and revealed something to me that changed the way I ministered. He said, "If you minister to my needs, I will use you to minister to their needs." And that's how it works. When you minister to the needs of the one who sent you, He will give you what you need to minister to the ones He sent you to.

The Holy of Holies, which was the most sacred compartment of the Tabernacle, was intended to represent the Throne room of God. The Ark of the Covenant is the only piece of furniture in the Holy of Holies, represented God's Throne. We see this picture when we read the sixth chapter of the Prophet Isaiah. God declares that He would meet with Moses between the faces of the Cherubim which signifies the Throne of God being surrounded by six six-winged angels. The reason that only two angels are on the Mercy seat, is because two is the number of agreement. And all six angels are in perfect agreement with God and one another. The reason they have six wings is because six is the number of Man, because Man was created on the sixth day. And God wants us to see that just like the six Angels with six wings are flying around the throne, constantly singing the praises of God so mankind was created for his life to revolve around the throne.

So, the Ark missing from the Temple, is symbolic of the Lord no longer having a seat of authority in His own house. It is a tragedy when the very thing missing from the House of the Lord is the presence of the Lord of the House! That's why John's ministry was in the Wilderness. Because God had to raise up a voice that was not confined within the walls of a religious establishment that didn't even realize that God's presence was missing. But I hear a prophetic voice crying in the Wilderness again. It declares to the religious establishment, "The Ark is missing, the glory has departed, but the Kingdom of Heaven is getting ready to invade the earth, and the Alien King is taking back what belongs to Him!"

Is Ecclesia Attracting Her Heavenly Husband?

No matter how hard and long you pray for it to happen, the Kingdom of God will not draw closer to you if you are not living a life that's attractive to the King. The only way to attract the Kingdom is to do the things that attract the King.

Revelation 21:2 NLT

"And I saw the holy city, the New Jerusalem coming down out of heaven from God, prepared like a Bride beautifully adorned for her husband."

Revelation 21:9-10 NLT

⁹Then one of the seven angels who held the seven bowls containing the seven last plagues came and said to me, "Come with me! I will show you the bride, the wife of the Lamb." ¹⁰So he took me in the Spirit to a great, high mountain, and he showed me the holy city, Jerusalem, descending out of heaven from God.

The Bible compares the Holy City, the New Jerusalem, which we know to be a representation of the Church, to a bride. What this passage of scripture communicates to us is that God does not view His Church as a Church He started, but as the bride He married.

It's interesting that at the end of the very last book of the Bible, God is not referring to The Church as, "The Church," He's referring to the Church as His bride. That's why my goal is to get people to begin to see things as God sees them. And more specifically see ourselves as He sees us. The reason that the Church only strives to be the Church is because She only sees herself as "The Church," instead of as His bride.

Our potential for intimacy with God would be far greater if we no longer viewed ourselves as just a Church He anointed, but as the bride He's in love with. The reason we lack an intimate relationship with God is because Churches don't get intimate, but brides do. I understand that this language sounds a little creepy, or maybe Even a lot creepy, cringy, and even weird to some. Especially because some circles have taken this concept way too far. So let me be very clear:

As a child of God, I am not the bride of Christ, And Jesus is not my heavenly husband. As a heterosexual male, I have no desire to entertain this word picture of being the bride of Christ, as it pertains to me. And let me also make it abundantly clear that this word picture does not apply to individual Christian women either. I've heard of women having ceremonies where they get married to Jesus, and refer to themselves as the bride of Christ, and refer to Jesus as their husband. That is not what God intended when he called his church the bride of Christ.

No one individual believer is the bride of Christ, but rather the Church, corporately, as a whole, is symbolic of Christ's bride, and Christ is symbolic of her husband. It's a metaphor that gives us a picture of a deeper, spiritual truth. So when I use words like intimacy to describe Christ's relationship with His Church, I'm not referring to anything that is physical or sexual in nature. I am rather referring to intimacy in its truest meaning, to share closeness, friendship, and love.

When God thinks of His Church, He does not think religiously, He thinks relationally. The reason that God formed a living man from the dust of the ground instead of a religious monument is because He knew that the most important thing for Him to have in the Earth was not a religion, but a relationship.

There is something known to theologians as the like as principal. What it means is that whenever you see the words like or as in the Bible, you have to pay attention to what comes after the word like or as in order to understand what the thing being talked about is like. For example, Psalm 1:3 referring to the blessed man, says he will be "...like a tree... planted by the rivers of water." If we apply the like as principal to this particular scripture we will ask ourselves the question, what is a tree that is planted by the rivers of water like?

Whatever answers we come up with is what we apply to what a blessed man is like. The scripture goes on to tell us what he is like. Like the tree, he brings forth fruit in his season, his leaf will not wither, and whatever he does will prosper. But there are things the scripture doesn't say that can be inferred from the like as principle. Such as, a tree planted by the rivers of water is nourished constantly by the flowing streams. So a blessed man is also nourished constantly by the flow of the Spirit and word of God in his life. If the blessed man is symbolic of the tree, then the rivers of water is symbolic of the flow of the Spirit and word of God. This passage doesn't explicitly say that, but it is inferred.

Revelation 21:2 says that the New Jerusalem is *"prepared like a Bride beautifully adorned for her husband."* It tells us how a bride is prepared. It says, "beautifully adorned..." But in order to fully apply the like as principle to this text we must delve a little deeper, and ask the question, How does a bride really prepare for her husband? The day, my wife and I got married was a rainy, but wonderful day. I cried like a broken-hearted little schoolgirl when those medieval like sanctuary doors opened, and her father escorted her down the aisle of that old-fashioned traditional Church in Powder Springs, Georgia. As they walked toward me, it was as if the different colors of the sun, beamed through the stained-glass windows, and danced to the music in the atmosphere above our heads. She was radiant, decked out, and stunning! When I read this Scripture, I think about that day.

If there is any day that a woman goes all out, and is expensively excessively and extravagantly adorned, it's her wedding day!!! She doesn't cut corners, hold back, or pinch pennies on this day. She's been thinking about it her entire life. It's the one day every woman gets to look like, feel like, and be treated by everyone like a real live princess.

The reason that God calls the Church His bride, as well as His wife is because He wants His wife, Ecclesia, to always prepare herself for Him like a bride prepares herself for her husband on her wedding day. God intends for His wife to constantly remain like His bride in the sense that she always expensively, excessively, and extravagantly prepares herself for Him!!! He wants her to expensively, excessively, and extravagantly decorate her life with the glorious jewels of obedience, surrender and worship that keeps Him as attracted to her as He was when she first said I do.

Is the Church today, as the bride of Christ, preparing herself for Christ, like a bride, prepares herself for her bridegroom, making sure, that her everyday life is attractive to her heavenly husband? I'm not talking about the external beauty of high steeples, stained glass windows, bright lights, and electric guitars. I'm talking about the internal beauty of a repentant heart and consistent prayer life. God didn't tell Moses to build the Tabernacle from the outside in; He told him to build it from the inside out. Man entered the Tabernacle from the outside. God entered the Tabernacle from the inside. The order of man is from the outside in. But the order of God is from the inside out!

1 Samuel 16:6-7 NLT

⁶When they arrived, Samuel took one look at Eliab and thought, "Surely this is the Lord's anointed!" (Outside in) ⁷The Lord told Samuel, "Don't judge by his appearance or height, for I have rejected him. The Lord doesn't see things the way you see them. People judge by outward appearance, but the Lord looks at the heart." (Inside out)

The most significant part of the Tabernacle was the part that was the most hidden. That was the part that God was most attracted to; the hidden part, the secret part; the part that wouldn't be seen by human eyes. That's the part of man that God is most fascinated with: the hidden man, the secret man, the part of man that cannot be seen by human eyes.

1 Corinthians 6:19 NLT

Don't you realize that your body is the temple of the Holy Spirit, who lives in you . . .

The Ark of the Covenant in the Holy of Holies is a representation of what the life of the believer should look like. Whatever it was that attracted the Presence of God to the Ark of the Covenant and The Holy of Holies is the same thing that's going to attract the Presence of God to us. Here's what I believe it was. It represented a carefully prepared secret place where God's presence alone was continually welcome. It communicated to God that this is a place that is deliberately built for no human activity.

It was built exclusively for the Presence of God! The thing about the Holy of Holies that made it so attractive to God is that it was the only part of the Tabernacle that was made exclusively for His presence! In Exodus 25:22, God said, *"From there I will give you my commands..."* In other words, God's voice is best heard in the environment His people create to attract His Presence.

So, if you're having trouble hearing the voice of God, it's probably linked to the fact that you have not created an environment in your life that is attractive to His presence. Or you have not caused your life to become an environment that is attractive to His Presence. You're not prepared like a bride! Before we had kids, my wife and I tried to have at least two date nights a month. Now with a five-year-old and an eight-year-old, we're fortunate if we get to have one date night every other month.

But when we do, we both dress up, then go out and have a good time with one another. Sometimes, she'll try on two different outfits, model them for me, and ask me which one I like the most. Though she looks great in all her outfits, the one that I like the most is the one she wears. Now imagine if she modeled a black dress and then a blue dress, and I chose the black one, but she decided to wear the blue one instead. I might not have a problem with that if she really preferred the blue dress. But if she said, "Rohan, I know you like the black dress, but your friend

Bobby really likes it when I wear this blue dress. So, I'm going to wear it for him." We would have a serious problem. Because I would want to know why she is more interested in wearing what another man wants her to wear than what I want her to wear.

The Church today is like a woman who dresses up for everybody else except for her husband. We garnish our lives with everyone else's opinions about what matters instead of decorating ourselves with God's word.

Christ - "You know I really love when you completely surrender to me in worship."

Ecclesia - "I know, Lord, but I've got to be reserved because everyone else likes when I'm dignified."

Christ - "But your repentant heart and radical worship is what attracts me."

Ecclesia - "I understand that, but everyone else gravitates to me when I have a more philosophical and laid-back approach to life. Thank you for saving me, but your demands are a little much for me right now. Maybe a few years from now, when I'm a more mature Christian, I can start dressing up in the kind of lifestyle that attracts you."

1 Peter 3:3-5 NLT

"³Don't be concerned about the outward beauty of fancy hairstyles, expensive jewelry, or beautiful clothes. ⁴ You should clothe yourselves instead with the beauty that comes from within, the unfading beauty of a gentle and quiet spirit, which is so precious to God. ⁵ This is how the holy women of old made themselves beautiful..."

Though this Scripture has a literal application, it also has a spiritual application. The literal application is about modesty and decency as children of the King.

Today, we are so afraid of being labeled as legalists that we no longer teach appropriate attire for children of God. If you are a Christian, you should not be dressing in a manner that provokes lust. Especially if you are serving in the house of the lord. We are ALIENS! We are a part of the culture of the Kingdom of God. We don't get to sacrifice holiness on the altar of fashion. My wife is very fashionable and careful not to dress in a manner that draws unnecessary attention to herself.

It's almost as if the Church doesn't care about this anymore. But pastors need to start preaching about it again. We've gone from one extreme to another. We've gone from robes that covered us from head to toe, to preachers in the pulpit wearing low-cut shirts and flexing their biceps. We've gone from women in the pulpit, who were so covered up, you couldn't recognize them, to women on stage whose jeans are so tight, most of the men can't focus on the worship service.

But this passage of scripture is not just literally about how women of God ought to dress. I believe it also has a spiritual and metaphoric connotation for the bride of Christ. Here is how I interpret it metaphorically:

"Don't be concerned with the outward beauty of a big Church building and the cosmetics of Christianity. Don't be obsessed with huge quires, nice suits, big hats, bright lights, screaming guitars, large crowds, fancy cars, big bank accounts, and high steeples. You should clothe yourself instead with the beauty that comes from within. A spirit drenched in the waters of humility and totally dependent on your Husband, who is Christ. This is how the early Church made herself beautiful for her heavenly Husband."

Do we live an extravagant life of obedience, surrender and worship, or are we spiritually dull, boring, and unattractive to the God, we're in relationship with? Does your life excite God, or are you a spiritual turn-off? No one wants to be in a relationship with someone who just wants to sit around and do nothing but look around. That's boring and unattractive! It's possible to love someone and yet be bored with their uneventful lifestyle and turned off by their unattractive qualities.

How boring and unattractive we in the modern Church must be to God! Instead of being interested in passionately pursuing His purposes, many of us are only interested in complaining about our lot in life. That's spiritually unattractive. Instead of adorning ourselves with a gentle and quiet spirit, we clothe our minds with anxiety and worry. We keep on the spirit of heaviness and refuse the garment of praise. We shun the oil of Joy and choose mourning for our companion. We're a plain Jane Church, who wonders why her majestic King can't take her into the celestial ballroom and dance with her to eternal love songs sung by a sea of angelic quires.

It hasn't occurred to the bride that maybe the reason her Heavenly Husband hasn't whisked her away into deeper dimensions of intimacy with Him is because she's rejected His regal robes of righteousness and chosen to remain dressed in the wretched rags of her own self-righteousness. Maybe God keeps His distance from the modern Church, not because He wants to, but because her unholy and idolatrous attraction to her made-up religious traditions has caused her to wreak with the stench of spiritual infidelity. Maybe He is not attracted to the way that she is no longer attracted to Him.

The early Church was exciting and adventurous to God. God could do exciting things through them because they were always available for His exciting exploits. They were passionate and intense. We're pessimistic and indifferent. They were adorned in the whole armor of God. We're either adorned with Bentley's bodyguards, and big bank accounts. Or bills, worries, and a Sunday-to-Sunday mentality. We in the pulpit have succeeded at being a profitable business, and those in the pews have succeeded at living an ordinary life. But we all have failed at being a beautiful bride. And isn't that what the Lord Jesus longs to see? He's not coming back for beautiful buildings, impressive budgets, and lavish banquet halls. Nor is He coming back for Sunday morning Saints. He's coming back for a bride without a spot, wrinkle, or blemish. He's coming back for a passionate, purposeful, and powerful Church! Because that's God's definition of a beautiful Bride! That's the Woman He envisioned when He was on the cross. She's beautiful in His eyes. Because she has used the garments, He gave her to prepare herself for Him!

Ephesians 5:25-27 NLT

[25]...He, (Christ), gave up His life for her, (the Church), [26] to make her holy and clean, washed by the cleansing of God's word. [27] He did this to present her to Himself as a glorious church without a spot, or wrinkle, or any other blemish. Instead, she will be holy and without fault.

Jesus did not give His life for His Church to present her to a denomination, organization, or institution. He gave his life for His Church so that He could cleanse her with His word, transform her into His likeness and present her to Himself. She is the object of His affection, and He longs to be with her.

Jesus never said, "These signs shall follow them that believe, in my name they will go to Church once a week, go to work every day, and try their best to be good wives, husbands, Moms, and Dads, until they eventually die and go to heaven." That's a boring existence! He said, "These signs shall follow them that believe in my name, they will cast out demons, heal the sick, speak with heavenly languages and earthly languages they never learned, raise the dead and impact the world." You're not just a wife and a mom or a husband and a dad. You're a supernatural wife, mother, husband, and father who loves your spouse and children and releases the anointing into their lives daily.

This is what attracts the King and His Kingdom! The King is attracted to our radical pursuit of Him because He likes being the center of attention. And when we make it all about Him, we will live the most exciting life because He will gladly make it all about us. This is how we become a society of aliens, able to minister to God and effortlessly intercede for our fellow man. It's a glorious portrait of what's possible when the Kingdom of Heaven comes to Earth.

LET US PRAY

Father God, I come before You on behalf of everyone who has prayerfully read the words of this book. From this day forward, may our hearts burn with a contagious passion for You! May the truth of the words You have given me to share in this work ignite a flame of righteous love within us. May we, as Your children, no longer spend our lives reasoning with Your will but rather responding to Your Spirit.

May the first invasion that takes place in our lives be an invasion of the awareness of Your overwhelming love for us. Grant us the grace to respond to that love with a heart of repentance and an insatiable thirst for Your Presence! Remind us that true repentance is making a commitment to exchange the way we think for the way that You think. Show us Your cross so that we may taste the sweetness of Your suffering and die to ourselves. Show us Your glory so we may awaken from the slumber of sin and sameness and live in Your resurrection power! Cleanse us from the guilt and stain of religion, and give us a heart that is completely surrendered to the process of becoming like You. Anoint us to invade the culture of this world system with Divine perspective and supernatural power that excommunicates the forces of darkness and establishes the Kingdom of Heaven in people's hearts. Fix our gaze on Heaven, and plant our feet on Earth so we can become gateways for astonishing outpourings of Your glory all over the world! May we go about each day with the awareness that our Kingdom is not of this world. And our agenda is to bring Earth under the government of Heaven.

May our evangelism be born out of intimacy with You, and give us the grace to live lives that attract Your attention, inherit Your favor, and advance Your agenda in this world. We thank and praise You for this in the precious name of our Lord and Alien King, Jesus Christ, Amen!

ABOUT THE AUTHOR

Rohan Peart was born in Kingston, Jamaica. He and his family migrated to the United States when he was only eight years old, where he grew up with his parents and two sisters in Baltimore, Maryland. Despite the corruption and chaos encircling his family in the bustling city, his parents raised him and his sisters with Christian values. Nevertheless, the hard times and fast-paced way of life soon proved to be too overwhelming for his Parents to bear. Though they were loving parents and devout Christians, they divorced when Rohan was twelve. They both remained a constant presence in their children's lives, but the devastation of a broken home eventually took its toll. Rohan found solace in taking to the streets of Baltimore and hanging out with the wrong crowd. Around this same time, a doctor informed his mother that Rohan had a learning disability that would prevent him from being able to comprehend as others could or even articulate himself properly. When she contended that she and his father believed Rohan was called to preach the gospel, the doctor told her in front of her son, "Don't fill his head with false hopes. He will never be able to articulate himself properly. Especially not in front of a group of people."

Though Rohan had been in special education since the third grade, those words were like daggers in both his and his mother's hearts. He felt generally misplaced in the world and misidentified by life.

But at 15 years old, something spectacular happened. His father, who appeared especially at peace and had an unusual glow on his face, came to visit him. He invited Rohan to go to church with him the next day. It was as if his father was on an assignment from heaven to bring his son to God. The following day, Rohan was escorted by his uncle to a little church on the outskirts of Baltimore, Maryland, where he wept his way to salvation. His life was radically transformed. At 16, Rohan visited his homeland of Jamaica, where he preached his first sermon, and quickly realized the heavy mantle of Ministry in his life. Against the doctor's diagnoses, he was miraculously able to do a lot more than just articulate himself properly. Since then, his burden to preach the gospel has ignited a passion for genuine revival in the hearts of many.

Rohan's non-traditional and uncompromising message ministers to many with a prophetic call to the heart of Worship. His passion is to help people encounter God's presence, and walk in their Purpose. He is the husband to his lovely wife of 16 years, Sheretha Peart. They have two small children, Shalom and RJ. He is the lead Pastor of Soul Winners Baptist Church in Memphis, TN.

Printed in the USA
CPSIA information can be obtained
at www.ICGtesting.com
LVHW020907210824
788840LV00015B/588